Uncle Arthur's Bedtime Stories

1

Arthur S. Maxwell

Activity Pages
by Cheryl Woolsey

Review and Herald®
Publishing Association
Hagerstown, MD 21740

This book was
Revised by Cheryl Woolsey
Revision edited by Gerald Wheeler
Art Direction by Bill Kirstein
Designed by Mark O'Connor
Cover Design by Helcio Deslandes
Cover art by Justinen Creative Group
Typeset: 12/16 Goudy

PRINTED IN U.S.A.

00 99 98 97 96   10 9 8 7 6 5 4 3 2 1

Artists participating in the illustration of this volume are: Harry Anderson, Harry Baerg, Mary Bausman, Robert L. Berran, Fred Collins, Wm. Dolwick, Thomas Dunbebin, Barbara Gibson, Arlo Greer, Russell Harlan, Joe Hennesy, Wm. M. Hutchinson, Justinen Creative Group, Art Landerman, Manning de V. Lee, Jackie Magee, Wendy Miller, Vernon Nye, B. Plockhorst, Jack White, and Charles Zingaro.

R&H Cataloging Service
Maxwell, Arthur Stanley, 1896-1970.
    Uncle Arthur's Bedtime Stories.
Activity pages by Cheryl Woolsey.

    I. Woolsey, Cheryl, 1956-   . II. Title.
III. Title: Bedtime Stories
    808.8

Library of Congress Catalog Card No. 96-19621

ISBN 0-8280-1007-2

Lesson Index

CONTENTS

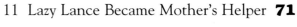

CONTENTS

Wayne's Secret

I WISH I could be a pirate!" said Wayne. "Everything is so boring, and I want to do something exciting."

"Yes," said Julie, "we've got to find something to do."

It was vacationtime. School had been closed for 10 days, and the children were getting tired of their toys. They wanted something new.

"Of course, we can't be pirates," said Julie, "because we'd get arrested."

"Of course," said Wayne, "but can't we think of something?"

"Let's think."

So they thought and thought. Neither of them spoke for several minutes. Then Wayne jumped to his feet.

"I've got it!" he cried. "Let's call ourselves the Surprise Package Company. I'll be the president, and you can be the secretary."

7

"All right," said Julie, willing to do anything her big brother suggested, "but what are we going to do?"

"Do? Why, give people surprises."

"What sort?"

"Oh, good ones, of course," said Wayne. "We'll find people who need things done for them, and then make them wonder how they happened. I think it would be lots of fun."

"So do I," said Julie. "Let's begin soon."

"OK. I'll make a list of things, and then we can decide what to do first."

Wayne found a pencil and paper and made his list.

"Now, look here," he said solemnly, "don't tell anybody what we are planning to do. It's a secret."

"Of course not," said Julie. "What do you think I am!"

That afternoon when Mother returned from town she put her grocery bags on the kitchen table. Then she dropped into a chair and stared. What a kitchen! She had gone to town right after dinner, leaving all the dirty dishes in the sink. Now they had disappeared. The kitchen had been cleaned up, everything was in its place, the table was all set for supper, and, yes, even the windows had been cleaned!

All was quiet and still. Nobody was in the house. What kind person could have done all this?

Wayne and Julie came in from the yard. Mom asked them whether Aunt Ruth had come by during the afternoon. Wayne said No, he didn't think so, but it did look as if someone had been busy.

"Well," said Mother, "isn't it just lovely! I have no more work to do today, and I can have a nice quiet rest this evening! I wonder who did it all?"

Mother opened a letter she had found on the doormat when she had come in. It read:

"The Surprise Package Company stopped by this afternoon on a little matter of business."

"I wonder what that means?" said Mother.

"I wonder," said Wayne.

"Let's have supper," said Julie.

And they did.

The next morning two children might have been seen going down the street leading to the little home of Mrs. O'Higgins. She was a poor, bedridden old lady many people seemed to have forgotten.

The boy, who was holding something in his right hand, knocked gently on the door. There was no answer. The boy peeped in at the window. Mrs. O'Higgins was fast asleep. Quietly opening the door, the boy walked in, followed by his sister. Tiptoeing across the room, the boy placed the package he was carrying on the table beside the bed and went out. In her excitement the little girl fell over the doorstep.

"Julie, be careful!" said the boy.

The noise had awakened the elderly lady.

"Who is that?" she called.

But the door was shut, and the two children were scampering away as fast as their legs would carry them.

Mrs. O'Higgins picked up the package. It contained three eggs.

"What a mercy!" she said to herself. "But who sent them?"

Looking at the wrapper, she read, "With love from the Surprise Package Company."

Frank Morley, a school friend of Wayne's, had the flu. Of course he had to stay indoors and was very miserable. From his bed he could see only a small patch of yard surrounded by a high brick wall.

One afternoon he was gazing vacantly out of the window when all of a sudden he saw a square box topple over the wall and slide down to the ground, held by a stout string.

"Mom, quick!" he called. "Someone dropped something in the yard."

Mother, all surprised, brought the box in, and Frank opened it. Inside were four smaller packages. One was labeled, "Open Monday"; the second, "Open Tuesday"; the third, "Open Wednesday"; the fourth, "Open Thursday."

Since it was Monday, Frank opened the first package. It was a box of paints—just what he had been longing for! Frank thought he had seen the box before but didn't know where. Inside the box were the words:

"With best wishes from the Surprise Package Company."

"What's that?" asked Frank.

Nobody knew.

On one occasion the Surprise Package Company was caught.

10

Wayne and Julie were paying a second visit to Mrs. O'Higgins.

This time they had brought some flowers, as well as eggs. As quiet as mice they crept in, placed their gifts on the table, and left.

The children were so eager to get in and out without waking up the elderly lady that they didn't notice a man sitting quietly in the next room. It was the doctor.

No sooner had the door closed behind the children than he went to the table, picked up the package, and read the note:

"With love from the Surprise Package Company."

"So this explains what Mrs. O'Higgins has been talking about!" he said. "And now I can understand what Frank Morley told me yesterday."

And this explains, too, why a few days later a letter arrived at the home of Wayne and Julie addressed to the Surprise Package Company and containing an invitation to lunch at Dr. Brown's.

The children had a wonderful time at the doctor's home, and there were two surprise packages that made up for all they had given away.

Of course, the children couldn't understand how the doctor had come to know about their secret, and he wouldn't say a word. It was all a delightful mystery. Wayne and Julie were as happy as children could be. Wayne said that it was much better than being pirates.

Muffin Mystery*

Perhaps you could make up a secret club like the Surprise Package Company! What kinds of things would you like to do to help people you know?

Muffins are quick and easy, and with a little jam in the center, they are a surprise package all in themselves. This recipe makes one dozen muffins you can use for some of your surprise projects. Turn on the oven to 400° F. Line the muffin tin cups with paper liners. Mix the following ingredients:

    1   egg, beaten
    ¾   cup milk
    ½   cup oil

Stir in the following ingredients until the flour is barely wet. The batter will be lumpy.

    2   cups flour   ⅓   cup sugar
    3   tsp baking powder   1   tsp salt

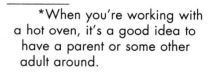

Fill the muffin cups half full. Put a teaspoon of jam on top of the batter, and then cover with batter. Bake the muffins for about 20 minutes, or until they are golden brown.

---

*When you're working with a hot oven, it's a good idea to have a parent or some other adult around.

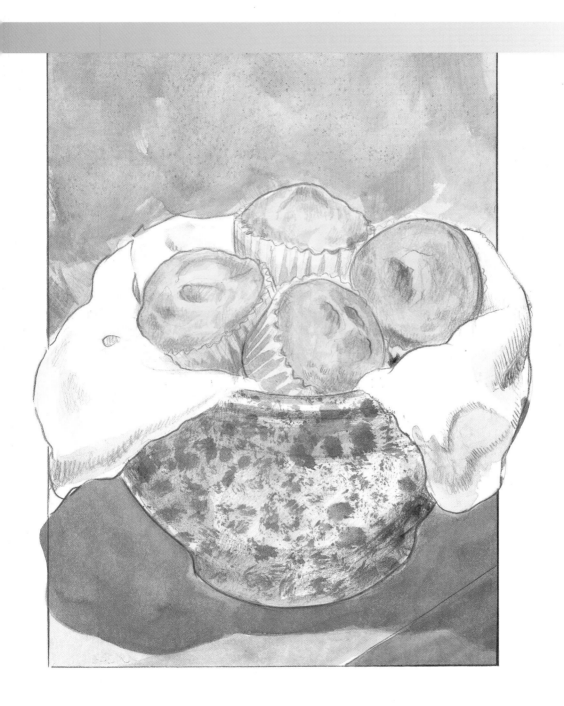

The Hollow Pie

ROBERT had the very bad habit of always taking the biggest and best of everything for himself. His brothers, Charlie and Ted, would call him all sorts of names for doing it, but that didn't seem to make any difference.

Mother was very sorry about it too, especially since Robert always disgraced the family by his greediness when they were invited out to eat. What could be done? Mother talked the matter over with her sister, who lived on the next street.

A few days later the boys were delighted to receive an invitation to dinner from their aunt. Remembering all the good things they had enjoyed there in times past, they looked forward to the party.

At last the day came and dinnertime arrived. The table was piled with good things. Robert looked longingly at the cupcakes, jellies, small pies, and chocolate candy.

14

Oh, my! he thought, *if only I could do something about this all by myself!* He looked at the wonderful spread of tasty dishes and made up his mind which of them he would choose when they were passed around.

Everybody sat down, and dinner began with bread and potatoes and greens in the usual way. But Robert soon got tired of that. He looked at the plate of small pies. He wanted that biggest one. Would he get it in time, or would Charlie get it first?

The pies were passed around. Charlie and Ted took small ones and opened them. *What wonderful centers they have!* thought Robert. *Now, if only I can get that big one.*

Robert's turn came. The biggest pie was still there, and he took it eagerly. But what a disappointment! As he cut through the top, the whole pie collapsed. It was hollow! Poor Robert! Tears filled his eyes, but no one seemed to notice what had happened. He ate the crust as bravely as he could and said nothing.

The cupcakes were passed around. Robert thought he was quite justified in taking the biggest this time, since there had been nothing in his pie. But something was wrong with his cake. It looked all right outside, but the center was bitter.

What can be the matter? thought Robert. Auntie was such a good cook. The others didn't seem to be having any trouble at all. *It isn't fair,* thought Robert, but he didn't dare say anything for fear the others would laugh at him.

Nobody seemed to notice Robert's unhappiness, and no one passed him anything to make up for his bad luck. In fact, the others all seemed to be thoroughly enjoying themselves

The chocolate candy came next, and by this time Robert was getting desperate. "I'll have to make up for lost time by taking those two big beauties in the center," he said to himself as he removed the two largest, best-looking pieces of candy from the plate.

"Ugh!" said Robert, groaning inwardly and blushing all over with disappointment. "What a horrible taste!" Swallowing one with difficulty, he tried the other to take the taste away, only to find it worse.

On the way home Charlie said something to Robert about what a splendid dinner they had had.

"Splendid *what?*" said Robert.

"I thought you weren't enjoying yourself," said Charlie; "you looked uncomfortable. What was the matter?"

"Matter?" said Robert. "Everything I took was bad, even when I took what looked best every time."

"Maybe that was the problem, Robert," said Charlie knowingly. "I think if I were you I'd leave the biggest and best-looking things for somebody else next time."

That night Robert stayed awake quite a long time. There were two reasons. One was a pain under his pajama top, and the other the advice Charlie had given him. He put two and two together and at last decided that the best and safest course for him would be to follow Charlie's suggestion in the future.

Patti Pays Up

PATTI was staying with her grandma, and early one afternoon Grandma suggested that they go shopping together. Patti was delighted. Very soon the two were on their way.

They went into the neighborhood grocery store and were met with a cheery "Good afternoon" from Mrs. Green, the smiling clerk behind the counter. Grandma went over to talk to her and buy the things she had written down on her list while Patti wandered around looking at all the beautiful things for sale.

A pile of fresh brown loaves of bread and rows of tempting cakes and pies lay in a glass cabinet in one corner. Cartons of milk and packages of butter and cheese were stacked in the refrigerator. All sorts of bright-colored cartons were piled up on shelves, and baskets of fruit and vegetables stood in the center of the floor. All the food made a very pleasant picture, and the mix-

19

ture of delicious aromas made Patti very, very hungry.

Maybe you know how it feels to be 5 years old, to take a long walk, and then go into a store full of food. Well, Patti felt just like that.

Several baskets filled with big luscious blackberries were sitting right in front of her. How Patti loved blackberries! She could never get enough of them, and here were more blackberries than she had ever seen before.

She put out her hand to take one, but a little voice inside her seemed to say, "No, Patti, you mustn't do that; that would be stealing." But the berries looked so delicious that she felt she *had* to take one. After all, she thought, there were so many, many berries that nobody would ever notice if she took just one.

So Patti didn't listen to her conscience. Instead, she put out her hand and took just one blackberry. But that one tasted so good that she decided to take another one. How sweet it was!

Then, since there seemed to be just as many left in the basket as there had been before, she took one from another basket. And another. In fact, she was just settling down to a real meal of blackberries when she heard a familiar voice from the other side of the store.

"Patti! Patti! Where are you?" called Grandma.

"Here I am, Grandma," answered Patti, wiping her hands on the back of her dress and hurrying around the pile of baskets.

"Come along, dear," said Grandma. "We're all ready to go home now. Would you like to carry one of the bags? How good you have been all the time Grandma has been shopping!"

Patti blushed a little as she took the bag Grandma handed to her. Then they opened the door and went out.

As they walked along Grandma suddenly stopped.

"Patti," she said, "look at me!"

Patti looked up, trying to appear as innocent as possible.

"What are those black marks on your face, Patti?" asked Grandma.

20

"What black marks?" asked Patti.

"All around your mouth. Not quite black, but blackish red."

"I don't know," said Patti, although if she could have seen her dirty face, she would have confessed what had happened right away.

"Patti, you have been eating blackberries," said Grandma. "Haven't you?"

Patti's head went down. "Just a few," she said.

"Where did you get them?" asked Grandma.

"In the store," said Patti.

"Did Mrs. Green say you could have them?"

"No."

"Do you mean you took them without asking?"

"Yes."

"That was the wrong thing to do," said Grandma, "and I am very sorry. Come along, let's go home, and we'll talk about it."

Patti began to cry, and it was a very sad walk they had together, so different from the journey they had taken to the store just a little while before.

After they went inside the house, Grandma took Patti on her lap and told her how very wrong it is to take things that belong to other

people. It is breaking the commandment which says, "Thou shalt not steal." She also told Patti that there were two things she could do to make it right. One was to ask God to forgive her and the other was to go to Mrs. Green, pay her for the berries she had eaten, and tell her how sorry she was that she had taken them.

"I don't mind asking God to forgive me," said Patti, crying, "but I don't want to ask Mrs. Green."

"I know it's hard," said Grandma, "but it's the only way. Now go and find your purse."

"You mean I have to pay for the berries myself?"

"Yes," said Grandma.

"But it will take all my money," said Patti.

"You should make it right even if it takes all the money you have," said Grandma. "But I don't think the berries will cost that much. In fact, I believe a quarter should pay for everything you ate."

"A whole quarter!" said Patti. "Do I have to give Mrs. Green a whole quarter?"

"Yes," said Grandma. "And the sooner we go back to see her the better. Are you ready?"

Patti wiped her eyes with the backs of her hands. Holding her quarter tightly, she set off for the grocery store with Grandma.

How far away it seemed. Patti dragged one weary foot after the other! But at last they reached the store. Her heart beating hard, Patti went inside.

"What! Back again so soon!" exclaimed Mrs. Green. "Did Grandma forget something?"

"No," said Patti slowly, "I did."

"You did!" said Mrs. Green. "What did you forget?"

"Mrs. Green, er—er—I—er—er—please, I forgot to pay for the blackberries I ate. And—er—er—please, Grandma said they're worth a quarter. So I've brought it out of my very own money and—

22

er—er—please, I'm very sorry I didn't ask you about them first."

Patti put the quarter on the counter, turned around, and ran for the door. Opening it, she dashed outside to where Grandma waited. They started home, but had not gone far when they heard Mrs. Green calling.

"Patti!" she said. "Will you please come back for a minute?"

Very slowly Patti returned to the store, as if expecting to be scolded.

"You forgot something else," said Mrs. Green, smiling, and handing her a paper bag.

"No," said Patti, "I didn't leave that."

"But it's for you, anyway," said Mrs. Green. "Just something good for your supper." Then she patted her on the arm and told her to go on home. Patti thought she saw tears in her eyes, but she wasn't quite sure, and she couldn't think why. She ran back to where Grandma stood waiting.

"Look what she gave me!" Patti cried. "Grandma, look!"

Grandma looked. It was a big delicious-looking doughnut with jam inside.

"Aren't you glad you went back and made things right?" asked Grandma.

"Am I!" exclaimed Patti.

"It's always the best thing to do," said Grandma.

Fruit and Vegetable Prints

The beautiful fruits and vegetables in a grocery store aren't just good to eat—they have other interesting uses. You can design wrapping paper and cards with prints from fruit and vegetables. Cut peppers or oranges in half then dip the cut surface in the paint. Squeeze most of the juice out of the orange half first, but be careful not to break the sections. You can make cross cuts in pieces of celery or carrots to print crescent shapes, circles, or ovals. Try printing a border to frame a picture or a poem you wrote.

For variation, try using colored paper with white or colored tempera paint for making the prints.

Nita's Wish

SCHOOL had let out for the holidays. Everyone was looking forward to Christmas Day. How slowly the days seemed to pass! It seemed as if Christmas would never come. Outdoors it was too cold to play, and indoors the children always seemed to be getting in Mother's way.

"Oh, what *can* we do?" said Nita to her sister Elena.

"Let's write that letter to Santa Claus we were going to send him."

"If you want to," said Nita. "Do you know what? I think Santa Claus is Daddy dressed up."

"Do you?"

"Yes. Last Christmas I kept one eye open until someone came into my room to fill my stocking, and I'm sure it was Daddy in his bathrobe."

"But let's write the letter anyway," urged Elena.

"Oh, yes, that will be fun, won't it? What shall we ask him to send us?"

"Let's get some paper and a pencil first, so we won't forget anything."

"I'll run and get some," said Nita, and off she went, coming back in a few minutes with enough paper for a long letter.

Since Elena had just learned to write, the girls agreed that she should write the letter, and Nita would tell her how to spell the words.

"Before you begin, let's try to think of what we would like most," said Nita.

So they talked the matter over very seriously, and decided that they wanted a large number of things. Elena was sure she needed a box of paints, a baby doll, a doll buggy, a ball, lots of candy, oranges, apples, and a music box. Nita had bigger ideas. She wanted a bicycle, some good books with pictures in them, a big box of chocolate candy, and above all, a doll that could talk and move its eyes.

"I really don't think he will be able to carry them all," said Nita.

"Oh, I do," said Elena. "He has a big bag."

"Yes, and there is no harm in putting them all down."

So they did. Carefully little Elena wrote the letter, underlining all the things they wanted most. At last the letter was finished and ready to be placed in an envelope. Nita read it over, all the way from "Dear Santa Claus" down to "Hoping to see you soon." Then she gave a little sigh, and put it on the table.

"What's the matter?" asked Elena.

Nita was silent a moment. Then she said, "I think it is a rather selfish letter."

"Why?"

"Because we've asked things only for ourselves. There's not one thing for anyone else."

"That's right. What should we do? Should we write it all over again?"

"Oh, no, that would take too long. Why not add a postscript?"

"What's that?"

"Just a few words at the bottom."

"All right. What shall we say?"

"I would like to see some of the poor children at school get some nice things like those we have asked Santa Claus to send us."

"So would I."

"There's Misty Gomez," said Nita. "She's such a nice girl, but her mother is so poor that I don't suppose she will get any Christmas presents at all—or nothing worth much."

"Really?"

"I don't suppose so."

"Then let's ask for something nice for her. I'm sure she'd like a pretty doll, too."

"Yes," said Nita, "put that down. Then the letter will be all right, I think."

So Elena carefully added the words "Please see that Misty Gomez gets a beautiful doll." Then they folded the letter, put it in the envelope, stuck an old stamp on it, and asked Mother to mail it.

Christmas morning came, and with it all the glorious fun of emptying stockings and examining the presents that were piled up under the tree. Nita and Elena were as happy as children could be, shrieking with delight as they opened each package and found one of the things they had asked for in their letter. Of course, they didn't get *all* their requests, but they got enough to make them feel sure Santa had read their message.

But one thing was wrong, at least so far as Nita was concerned. She didn't say anything about it until she had opened all her packages. Then she began to look just a little bit worried. She turned all the tissue paper over again and again and then looked under the bed, even in the closet, but what she wanted most of all wasn't there.

"What's the matter, Nita?" asked Elena. "Don't you have enough presents?"

"Oh, Elena," said Nita, "I know I have some nice things, but *it* isn't here."

"What do you mean?"

"I *really* wanted a baby doll that says, 'Mamma.'"

"Maybe he took one to Misty Gomez instead of you."

"Maybe so," sighed Nita. "But I didn't mean that he should give a doll to her instead of me."

Then Nita thought about what she had just said and realized how selfish it was. She had all these beautiful presents, and she wondered whether Misty had anything. All day she felt unhappy about it, and while she was playing with her new toys she kept thinking, *Should I have taken Misty some of my things?*

In the evening Nita and Elena went to a party that was being given by the woman next door. Several other little girls had also been invited, and they had a fine time together. After refreshments—and what good food it was!—they all went into another room where a beautiful Christmas tree stood, covered with pretty shiny decorations and little colored lights. It was a very thrilling sight.

But the thing that captured Nita's attention most was a beautiful doll lying among all the other gifts placed beneath the tree. Her heart beat fast as she thought that perhaps now her greatest wish would be granted. The children played all kinds of games around the tree, and at last the presents were distributed. Only one thought was in Nita's mind. Who was going to get the doll? Impatiently she waited and waited while every other child received a gift. Now there was just one present left under the tree—the doll!

"This," said the woman, "is for—"

"Nita," said all the children, for they saw that she had not been given a gift from the tree so far.

Nita blushed and jumped up from her seat. Taking the doll from the woman, she hugged it tightly to herself.

Then a strange thing happened. Nita was walking back to her seat when suddenly she pointed to the window and cried, "Oh, look! look!"

Everybody looked, but there was nothing to be seen. The shades were up, but everything was dark and still outside.

"What was it?" cried all the children.

"It was Misty Gomez. She was looking in at the window, and I'm sure she was crying. Oh, I must go and find her!"

Without another word Nita rushed to the front door and ran out, not even waiting to put on her coat. Far down the street under a light Nita thought she saw a little figure.

"Misty!" she cried. "Misty! Come here."

But Misty went on, and Nita had to run the whole length of the block before she caught up with her little friend.

"Oh, Misty!" she panted. "I've brought you something. Please stop and take it."

Misty stood looking in amazement at the wonderful thing Nita held in her arms. It was a doll that could shut its eyes and say "Mamma."

"For me?" she said.

"Yes, yes, for you," said Nita. "I want you to have it most of all." Then she turned and ran back to the house, feeling happier than she had ever felt before.

That night as she went to sleep she remembered the note she had added to her letter to Santa Claus. How thankful she was that she had helped to answer it!

Who Was Jesus?

WHO WAS Jesus? A baby in Bethlehem? Yes. A carpenter's boy in Nazareth? Yes. A kind man who helped sick people? Yes. Jesus was all these things and much more.

Long before Jesus came down to this world as a baby in Bethlehem He lived in heaven. He was the One who created this world in which we live. He made the beautiful trees, the flowers, the hills, the valleys, the birds, the animals, and the fish in the sea.

All the angels loved Him and were delighted to do anything He asked. Everything was happiness and joy.

Why, then, you ask, if Jesus was so happy in heaven, did He come down to the world at all?

Because He loved the people here, and it made Him sorry to see so many dear little boys and girls growing up to be wicked men and women. True, it was a great sacrifice for Him to give up the joys of

35

heaven for the sorrows of earth, but He did it. He knew there was no other way to help people to live better, and no other way to save the little children for His kingdom.

But why did Jesus come as a little baby, and not as a grown-up man?

Jesus wanted to grow up like all other little boys and girls. He wanted to live like they live, so He could help them better.

Jesus the baby grew into Jesus the little boy, and He became Jesus the man of Nazareth, who went all over Palestine doing kind deeds and healing all the sick people who came to Him.

He taught the people many beautiful lessons, and told them how to live peacefully and happily together. It was Jesus who said that we should do the same kinds of things to others that we would like them to do to us.

"You have heard that it was said, 'Love your neighbor and hate your enemy.' But I tell you: Love your enemies and pray for those who persecute you" (Matthew 5:43, 44, NIV).

Not only did Jesus teach the people how to live, but He showed them how to live by the kind things He did for them, and all the people loved Him. That is, all except a few. There were some who were jealous because the people liked Him so much. Some didn't like the way He pointed out what they were doing wrong, and others didn't understand Him.

Some of the leaders plotted to kill Him. Think of it! Here was the Son of the great God of heaven, walking around with the people on earth, healing and helping them in every way He could, and yet some wanted to kill Him!

And these men managed to do just that. They lied about Jesus to Pilate, the Roman governor who ruled Palestine. Pilate knew the men were lying, but he was too much of a coward to stand up for Jesus. Instead he sent Him away to be crucified.

The Roman soldiers nailed Jesus by His hands and feet to a wooden cross in the cruelest possible way. Then they stood the cross up on a place called Golgotha, outside of Jerusalem.

There on the cross Jesus soon died, killed by pain and sorrow. When He was dead His friends came and took His body down and buried Him in a rock tomb belonging to a man called Joseph of Arimathea.

Why did Jesus let the wicked people kill Him?

That's how He showed everyone how much He loved them. He could have called all the angels of heaven to help Him fight those wicked men who nailed Him to the cross. But no, He was willing to die, because this was the only way to save us from our sins.

That is what the beautiful text means that says, "For God so loved the world that he gave his one and only Son, that whoever believes in him shall not perish but have eternal life" (John 3:16, NIV).

Jesus died and was buried, but He didn't stay dead. On the third day the disciples came to His tomb and found it open and empty. A little later Jesus met them, and they rejoiced that their beloved Master was alive once more.

For 40 days He stayed with the disciples telling them about the work He wanted them to do. They were to go out into all the world to tell everybody they met—men and women, boys and girls—how much Jesus loved them.

Then one day while He was talking with His disciples near Bethany, He slowly began to rise above them. He rose higher and higher into the air until at last, far up in the skies, "a cloud hid him from their sight" (Acts 1:9, NIV), and He was gone.

Though Jesus went back to heaven, He didn't forget the people He left behind on earth. He's never forgotten His children through all the long years that have passed since that time.

His love never changes. He is the same yesterday, today, and forever. He died when He was only a young man, and He never grows old. Since He was a boy Himself once, He knows just how to help other children today, rich or poor, sick or well, in all their problems and in all their temptations. He will never fail you if you trust Him. He is the children's Friend.

"There's a Friend for little children
    Above the bright blue sky;
A Friend that never changes,
    Whose love will never die.
Unlike our friends by nature,
    Who change with changing years,
This Friend is always worthy
    The precious name He bears."

The Nativity Scene

You can make a Nativity scene of baby Jesus, Mary, Joseph, and as many other characters in the story as you like. Use ¾-inch dowels, small painted wooden heads (found in a craft shop or molded out of dough), pipe cleaners, and scraps of material.

Fold a piece of white cloth to look like a baby's sleeping bag, and glue a small head near the top for baby Jesus. Cut the dowels into 2- or 2½-inch lengths. Round off one end of each dowel for shoulders, and glue on a head. Fold back each end of a 2-inch length of pipe cleaner for hands, and glue the middle of the pipe cleaner at the back of the head and shoulders.

Dress each figure appropriately. A small rectangle of material folded over each arm and glued together at the bottom makes sleeves. Choose heavier, contrasting material for a cloak. To make one, split a rectangle of material 4 to 5 inches long by 1½ inches wide to the center, where you should cut out a small circle for the neck. The opening can go in the front or in the back. Use silks and rich colors for the Wise Men, decorating them with sequins and plastic jewels. Fashion turbans for the Wise Men's heads, and glue gold braid down the front of their robes.

Those Prayers of Yours

DOES Jesus really hear and answer children's prayers?

Of course He does, and don't you ever let anybody try to make you think He doesn't. I'm quite sure, because, you see, so many children have told me about their prayers that have been answered.

One time Jesus was talking with His disciples about prayer, and He said, "Ask and it will be given to you; seek, and you will find; knock and the door will be opened to you" (Matthew 7:7, NIV).

Then He went on to say, "Which of you, if his son asks for bread, will give him a stone? Or if he asks for a fish, will give him a snake?" (verses 9, 10, NIV).

No Daddy would do that, you say. It would be a pretty cruel father who would give his hungry little boy a stone or a snake to eat.

Next Jesus added these wonderful words of love: "If you then, though you are evil, know how to give good gifts to your children, *how much more* will your Father who is in heaven give good gifts to those who ask him!" (verse 11, NIV).

It seems to me that in these simple words Jesus is trying to tell us that God loves us so much that there isn't anything, great or small, that He will not do for us, if it is for our good. We just need to ask Him for His help.

Let's keep saying our prayers, children, believing that God is more ready and willing to answer than we are to ask. If you need anything, even something that seems too big to ask for, don't worry. You can't surprise your Father in heaven. He loves you with an everlasting love—a love high as the heavens and deep as the sea. And if what you ask for might not be the right thing for you, or might hurt someone, He will give you something else that is even better. He will surprise you with the greatness of His goodness and His love.

Now don't get the wrong idea. God won't give us everything we ask for. Your mother doesn't, does she? If you were to ask her for a $10 bill to spend on candy, would she give it to you? I should say

not. And why not? Because she knows that so much candy would probably make you sick.

So don't be surprised if now and then you don't seem to get an answer to your prayers. When that happens ask yourself this question: Did I pray for something selfish? God loves to do what is good for us, but He doesn't want to spoil us any more than Mother does.

If you don't get an answer to a prayer right away, don't let yourself become sad or discouraged. If you are sure that what you want is good, keep on praying. God will answer your prayer at just the right time.

Remember to always let God make the final decision. When you pray, you might say something like "I only want You to do this for me if *You* want to do it." Then, whatever happens, you will be satisfied. If you trust God like this you will never be worried if the answer seems slow in coming or if it doesn't seem to come at all.

In the next story, and in other stories in these volumes, you will read amazing examples of answers to children's prayers. I have been collecting them for some time, and I know all the people in the stories. Of course I haven't given their real names, or the real places where the events happened, for they might not like that, but the stories are true.

When you read the first one, I am sure you will say, "That was remarkable." When you read the second, you will say, "That was amazing." But when you have read them all, I believe you will say, "That makes me sure now that God does answer prayer."

Yet there is only one way to be perfectly certain, and that is to prove God for yourself. Ask Him for something—something that you really, truly need, or better still, something for someone else. Ask Him earnestly, seriously, confidently, and then wait and watch.

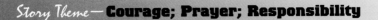

Story Theme— **Courage; Prayer; Responsibility**

Two Brave Firemen

THE TROUBLE couldn't have come at a worse time. Father was away from home. Mother was still on crutches as a result of a bad accident she had been in some weeks before. Nine-year-old David and 6-year-old Gordon were just getting over the measles, and Big Sister—well, she had left for college that very afternoon.

Suddenly, as David looked out of the kitchen window, he saw smoke rising from behind the barn. "Look," he cried to Gordon, "see that smoke? Whatever can be burning there?"

48

Then he remembered that the last thing Big Sister had done before she left was to carry out the hot ashes and dump them on the ash pile. She must have been in such a hurry she had spilled some on the dry grass.

"Fire!" he shouted. "Fire!"

"What's on fire?" called Mother from the next room, hobbling out on her crutches.

"Look, Mamma!" cried David. "The grass is on fire near the barn and the flames are spreading fast. See the smoke! Oh, what can we do?"

Poor Mother had never felt so helpless in all her life. Everything she owned was in danger, and yet with her injured foot she could do nothing.

"David, run for water, dear. Quick, quick!"

"Yes, Mamma," cried David, grabbing two pails and running to the stream, which was at least 50 yards away.

Gordon grabbed another pail and in a flash was following his

brother. Quickly they filled the pails, hurried back, and poured the water on the burning grass nearest the barn. Then back for more water, and back again to the fire.

But it seemed a losing fight. After all, how could two little boys with three little pails put out a great big fire?

"Keep it away from the gas tank!" cried Mother. "See, it's going that way."

It was. Nearer and nearer it crept to the precious store of gasoline Father used for his tractor. If that should catch fire, then the house, barn, and everything might burn down.

The boys were getting tired now. It was so far to the stream! And it seemed farther every time they went down to it. Still they ran as hard as they could, and with every step they kept praying that Jesus would help them put the fire out.

Back they came with water to save the gas tank. And they saved it—just in time. Of course, they couldn't hope to stop the fire from going across the field—not with their three little pails. But they tried—oh, so hard—to keep it from creeping over to the barn and the house. And they did! The farm was saved.

Just as things were at their worst and the boys were getting so tired that they felt they couldn't carry another pailful, the wind changed. It blew the fire down toward the stream where finally it burned itself out at the water's edge.

Was Mother proud of her two boys? I should say she was! And so was Father, when he got home and learned of all they had done.

As for David and Gordon, they told me that they were sure they managed to beat the fire because of the little prayer they had prayed so often as they hurried to and from the stream with their pails.

Important Names and Numbers

There are several names and numbers you need to know in case of an emergency. It's fun to practice them. Have someone pretend he doesn't know who you are. He should ask you your name. Can you say your first name as well as your last name? Can you give your house number and the name of your street? What about your telephone number?

It is also useful to know how to call an emergency number such as the police, if you need help. You can have fun decorating a card with the number on it, to put near the phone. If you have a play phone, pretend to call the emergency number and explain a pretend problem.

Remember to give your name, address, and phone number when you call the emergency number.

New Hearts for Old

SOME years ago I wanted a really good music system. Then one day I heard that a man was selling one of the finest stereo sets ever made because he was leaving the country. I went to see him, and as soon as I heard its beautiful tone I knew it was the one I wanted. We finally agreed on the price, and the stereo became mine.

Two days later a truck drew up at my house and two men staggered in with the beautiful new piece of furniture and placed it carefully in the corner of my dining room. I plugged it in and began to turn the various knobs on the radio.

There were grunts and squeaks and groans and roars and rattles, but no music. I could get nothing out of that beautiful cabinet but dreadful groans and shrieks. What could I do?

At last I called in a friend who understands radios. But the same

thing happened to him. As he turned the knobs, the set roared and rattled as before.

"How about your tubes?" he said after a while. In those days, radios used tubes which often got damaged. "I think they are worn out or have been jarred on the journey."

"If that's the trouble," I said, "let's get some new ones."

I'll never forget watching him take the old tubes out and put the new tubes in. Then he switched on the electric current again, turned the knobs ever so carefully, and—

Ah! Everything was different now. Out of the set came the most glorious music I had ever heard, distant and unearthly at first, but swelling into loud, majestic tones that fairly shook the house. My dream had come true, although before it was possible, the tubes had to be changed.

Whenever I think of that experience, my mind goes to that text in Ezekiel in which God says, "I will give you a new heart and put a new spirit in you; I will remove from you your heart of stone and give you a heart of flesh" (Ezekiel 36:26, NIV).

It seems to me that we are all very much like that stereo of mine—beautiful on the outside, but bad on the inside. Or we might be like a beautiful doll that was given to a little girl one time. Just as she was hugging the doll and kissing its pretty face, its eyes fell in! And then it looked so ugly that she felt she could never love it again.

Sometimes little boys and girls are like this. Perhaps Mother dresses her children in nice new clothes. They look so clean and spotless that people almost think they are little angels from heaven. But then the children begin to quarrel, and there is such a noise and such a squabbling that they become more like monkeys or wildcats than children—let alone angels!

It isn't just clothes and looks that make people beautiful. Lots of little girls with lovely curly hair can be as cross as bears when they can't have their own way. And many little boys look very fine in new suits, but they are as stubborn as mules when they feel like it.

Have you ever read the story of David, the brave, honest little shepherd boy? The Bible tells us that he had a beautiful face, and he was beautiful inside too, because he had a good heart.

God chose David to be king. "The Lord does not look at the things man looks at. Man looks at the outward appearance, but the Lord looks at the heart" (1 Samuel 16:7, NIV).

As long as our hearts are stony, we are like the radio with old tubes inside. It will be impossible to get any good music out of us. Stony hearts produce nothing but grumbling and growling, naughty words and sullen muttering, and everything that is unkind and unholy.

If you hear a boy being disrespectful to his father, or cross with his brother, or rude to his mother, you know that he has a stony heart and needs to have it changed. Or if you hear a girl grumbling about her food, or her clothes, or her friends, or saying cruel, cutting words, you can be sure that she needs a new heart.

It's the failure to get a new heart that causes all the trouble. Why don't we do it? It doesn't cost anything at all. God has promised to do it for free. Look at the text again. Notice what God says:

"I will give you a new heart and put a new spirit in you."

"I will remove from you your heart of stone and give you a heart of flesh."

God's offer is perfectly plain. Every one of us can ask Him for a new heart. And if we do, what a change will come over us! Mom won't know us, and Dad will hardly be able to believe his ears. There will be such beautiful music—such loving words, such tender sympathy, such gentle answers, such willingness to help and lift and share—that our home will seem like a little heaven on earth.

The Two Carolines

CAROLINE Herman was a very nice little girl in many ways. She had pretty hair and big blue eyes, and when she was all dressed and ready to go to school you would have thought, to look at her, that there wasn't a nicer little girl in all the world.

Caroline loved her schoolteacher very much. By the way she acted, it seemed as if she loved her teacher more than she loved her own mother. She would take her teacher flowers and other pretty things, and of course her teacher, seeing only the school Caroline, thought she was always a very good girl.

But there were two Carolines. One was the home Caroline, and the other was the school Caroline. The home Caroline was a cross, pouty, grumbly, growly, disobedient Caroline, very different from the Caroline that everybody saw outside and thought was such a nice little girl. The home Caroline was left on the doorstep every morning

58

and picked up every afternoon when the school Caroline came back.

Mother was worried almost to tears over her two Carolines. What could she do?

One day the school Caroline came home and changed suddenly on the doorstep, as usual, into the home Caroline. After a while Mother called, "Caroline, will you please go to the store and buy some groceries? Here is the list."

"No, don't want to, I'm tired," snapped the home Caroline. However, she finally decided to go under protest.

While she was gone, a visitor came to see Mrs. Herman to plan for the next parent-teachers' meeting, and was invited to stay for dinner.

"Just make yourself at home in the living room," said Mrs. Herman, "while I do a little in the kitchen. You can write at my desk and I'll leave the door open so we can talk."

In a few minutes Caroline came into the kitchen, slamming the back door and grumbling about the heavy groceries. "Here are your old things," she said, throwing them down on the floor. "Now I'm going out to play."

"But I'm tired," Mother said. "Wouldn't you like to help me finish my work?"

"No, I don't want to."

"Well, please set the table for dinner."

"Don't want to."

"But you must do something to help me. Please set the table, Caroline."

"Oh, I hate setting the table," said Caroline, making a face that would almost frighten anyone. Grumbling, she pulled out the table-cloth from the drawer and spread it out in a rough-and-tumble sort of way. Then she brought out the knives and forks, scattered them among a few dishes, and prepared to walk off.

Mother looked displeased, but didn't say anything until Caroline was about to go. Then she said, "Caroline, set an extra place at the table. We are having a visitor for dinner tonight. In fact, you might

speak to her now. She's in the living room."

Startled, Caroline looked around and noticed that the living room door was open.

"But, Mother dear"—her tone had suddenly changed—"the table is not set for visitors."

"No, but it is set for Mother."

"But, Mother, I want to fix it better."

"It is too late now. We can't keep our visitor waiting. Please call her in."

Trembling a little, Caroline went into the living room.

"Mother says, Will you please—"

She stopped. It was her teacher!

"Oh, Teacher, have you heard all I have been saying? Oh, dear!" cried Caroline, bursting into tears.

"I am sorry my Caroline is not the same at home as she is at school," said Teacher.

"Oh, I'm so sorry!" wept Caroline. "I won't ever be so naughty again."

And to tell the truth, from then on, Caroline tried very hard to remember to be as nice at home as she was at school.

Bracheo Breakfast

Why not surprise your mom on an ordinary day with breakfast? Make it different by planning it around a theme such as clowns, flowers, or dinosaurs. If you don't have a tray, use the lid of a box (such as copy paper comes in). Decorate the tray several days ahead with paint, pictures, or ribbons. Write out your menu, using interesting names for the different food items, such as "Tyranta Toast" or "Freshly Squeezed Jolly Juice." Add some recorded music and make someone's day!

The Boy Who Ran Away From Home

ONCE upon a time there was a rich man who had two sons. The man was a good father and loved his boys very much. He was willing to do anything for them to make them happy, although,

like all fathers, he expected them to obey him.

Their home was well furnished and beautiful. They always had plenty to eat and fine clothes to wear. Out on their broad farmlands they had sheep and goats, cattle and perhaps horses—just what most boys would love to own.

But one of the boys wasn't happy. He didn't like the rules on the farm. He thought he would never really enjoy life until he got away from home.

He'd heard that out in the world there was plenty of money that was easy to get. In the big city he would be able to have all sorts of fun he would never be allowed to have at home. He would be free! No one would tell him, "Don't do this," or "Don't do that"! He would be a grown-up man, his own master.

The more the boy thought about it the more eager he was to

65

leave the old farm and go out on his own. He decided to tell his father what he wanted to do.

"Dad," he said, "I am tired of living around this old place. I want to go out and see the world. Please give me some money."

His father was upset, but knowing that the boy would never appreciate home until he had been away from it, he gave him some money and told him he could go.

The boy was excited. Quickly he packed up his belongings and started off.

I don't know how he felt the day he left. Perhaps he was a little sorry when he kissed his mother goodbye and when he waved to her for the last time as he passed out of sight. I'm sure his mother cried when he was gone, and his father did too.

That first night away from home must have been lonely for him. Perhaps he thought of going back, but in the morning his mind was full of the great future before him in the world. Just think of the

66

money his father had given him! He had never had so much in his life before! Imagine what he could do with it!

He reached the city and began to spend his money. He quickly made many friends, who were only too glad to help him spend it. He had a wonderful time, although he was doing many things that his father had told him were wrong.

"This is real life," said the boy. "This is what I have always wanted. I can do just as I like, and there's no one to stop me from anything. To think that I ever lived back on that old farm!"

But one day the boy discovered that his money was running out. He had not been paying much attention to money matters beyond spending it. Now he was shocked that the money he had brought with him was almost gone. His pockets were nearly empty.

His new friends soon discovered this. One by one they left him, until at last, when he was penniless, he found that he was friendless too. Not one of his friends was willing to lend him anything or even give him food.

He began to see that if he was going to keep himself alive he would have to go to work. But what work could he do? The only thing he knew anything about was farming, and he didn't know much about that.

So he went to a farmer and asked for work. The farmer offered him the job of feeding his pigs at very low wages.

A few days before, this boy had been strutting about the city like a rich kid living on his father's money. Now he was a pigkeeper on a farm. And he was so hungry he felt he could eat even the pigs' food.

Poor boy! He had run away from home to have a good time in the world, but he found out that the world can be a very cold, hard place. Though it feels good for a little while, it ends up costing a lot.

He had been too busy having fun to think much about his home, but as he sat with the pigs, he had plenty of time to think. Home! What a beautiful place it seemed! He would give anything to be there again! Just to see his father and mother once more! Oh, why had he wanted to run away?

Finally he made a decision. He would go back. His father might be angry with him, but he would tell him he was sorry and ask his forgiveness. He planned what he would say to his father when he got home. It ran like this:

"Father, I have sinned against heaven and against you. I am no longer worthy to be called your son; make me like one of your hired men" (Luke 15:18, 19, NIV).

So the boy started on his long walk back home.

But what had been happening at home all this time? The father had been miserable. His son had not written to him once. Somehow

he felt sure that the boy would get into trouble, and maybe that would bring him home again.

Many times a day the father would look up the road, hoping to see his son. Day after day he was disappointed. Then one morning he went to look again. Straining his eyes, he gazed long and earnestly up the road to where it went out of sight over the hilltop.

What was that? It must be someone moving down the road. Yes! And the person looked strangely familiar. It looked like his long-lost son. Could it be? Could it?

"I believe it's my boy," the father murmured to himself, straining his eyes still more. "It is! It is! He has come at last!"

Forgetting his age and everything else, the father was so happy he started to run, never stopping until he had reached his son.

"Father, I have sinned—" began the boy.

But his father scarcely heard. He was too glad that his son was home again. Putting his arms around his neck, he hugged and kissed him.

When they got to the house, he called a servant to bring some new clothes for the boy to wear instead of his rags. Then the father put on a big party to celebrate the happy event.

The boy's brother couldn't understand why all this fuss was made over a bad boy's return, but the father said, "For this son of mine was dead and is alive again; he was lost, and is found" (Luke 15:24, NIV).

That kind father represents God. He loves us all as His children. If we want to run away from Him, He will let us go, but He knows that if we do, we will be very unhappy.

All the time we are away from Him He will be looking and longing for us to come back. He loves us with an everlasting love, and is always eager to welcome us back home again with wide-open arms, and brings us close to His heart.

70

Lazy Lance Became Mother's Helper

I WOULDN'T like to say out loud that Lance was lazy, because he would be very offended; and I don't like to offend any-body. But I am afraid that was the truth.

No matter what it was that you asked Lance to do he would always reply, "I can't." For every job he seemed to have an excuse. If you asked him to bring in wood for the fireplace he would say, "I can't; it's too heavy." Or if you asked him to go on an errand he would say, "I can't; I'm too tired." Perhaps you would ask him to wipe the dishes. Then he would say, "I can't; that's a girl's job."

Of course, his excuses didn't mean much, and I am quite sure that the real trouble with Lance was just pure laziness. You see, he said "I can't" only when there was work to be done. He never said it

71

at playtime or when his friend came to the door and asked him to go bicycling or to play ball. Then it was always, "All right, I'll be with you in a minute."

Lance's mother told him many times that it wasn't fair that he never helped at all with the housework and yet was so ready to run off and play. But Lance was the same as ever the next day. Everything Mother said didn't seem to make any difference. One day, however, Mother had a bright idea.

The next morning Lance stayed in bed so long that he was late for school. Usually Mother would call him in time to get ready, but Lance would answer drowsily, "I can't get up; I'm sleepy."

This morning Mother let Lance get up when he liked, and that was very late. He was cross when he came downstairs and wanted to have his breakfast immediately. But there was none for him.

"Why didn't you get my breakfast?" he asked.

"I can't," said Mother with a curious smile. "I'm so tired."

Very angry, Lance ran off to school without any breakfast. He was so late that the teacher scolded him in front of the class, which made him crosser still.

On the way home for lunch he climbed a fence with some other boys, and when he came down his pants got hooked on a rusty nail. He finally managed to get free, but he left part of his trousers on the top of the fence. When he got home he wanted Mother to mend them right away.

"I can't," said Mother. "I'm too busy."

"You mean I have to go back to school like this?" asked Lance, pointing to the hole in his trousers.

"I'm afraid so," said Mother. And that's what he had to do.

When Lance got home from school that afternoon, he wanted his supper right away, since he hadn't eaten much that day. But there was nothing on the table. He was surprised, because he had been used to finding everything ready for him.

73

"You don't have supper ready," he said to Mother.

"No," said Mother, "I can't. I'm tired. I just didn't feel like it tonight."

"But I want to go out to play right after supper," said Lance.

"All right," said Mother, not stirring from her armchair and looking back at the book she was reading. "Go ahead. I don't mind."

"But aren't you going to get me any supper?"

"I can't; I'm tired."

Lance stormed out of the house and slammed the door. But as he was going down the street he began to think things over. Perhaps Mother *was* tired after all. Maybe she really did need someone to help her. Perhaps she really was too tired to get her own supper ready.

Lance stopped. He thought of the game of ball he was going to enjoy and then of his mother sitting at home too tired to get her own supper ready. He began to feel sorry that he had been so cross. He would go back.

Peeping through the kitchen window, Lance saw that Mother had gone to sleep in her armchair. Suddenly he realized that this was his opportunity to make things right. He really

was a good boy, even though he had that very strong habit of laziness where work was concerned.

Creeping into the kitchen on tiptoe, he washed the dishes as silently as he could. Still more quietly, he crept into the dining room and set the table. To be quite frank, this was the first time for many months that Lance had set the table, but he did a fine job of it. He put out all the nicest things he could find, brought in some flowers from the garden, and really made the table look as if someone extra special were coming to supper.

Then he noticed that he had forgotten to bring in the butter dish and went to get it. Unfortunately it was a little greasy and it slipped out of his hands, falling with a crash to the floor.

Mother awoke and jumped out of her chair as if something dreadful had happened. She had been dreaming about Lance, and the noise had come just as he had been getting into trouble. But her fears turned to joy as she saw the neatly set table.

"Well!" she exclaimed, "who would have believed you could set a table so nicely!"

They had a lovely meal together, and Mother never said a word about the broken butter dish all evening. Lance was so happy that he decided he really would help Mother more after this.

Just as they were finishing supper, there was a knock at the door and a boy's voice called out, "Come on, Lance, we're all waiting for you."

"Sorry, I can't come," said Lance. "I'm going to help Mother this evening."

But Mother overheard, and she came running to the door. "It's all right, Lance, this time. You can help me tomorrow."

Overjoyed, Lance ran off, and I can tell you that was the best game of ball he ever played!

Sweeping

You can learn how to do a good job of sweeping with just a little practice. First, you will need a broom just your size. Buy a lightweight broom at the grocery store. The broom should stand just a bit shorter than you are. You may need to have someone help you cut off a too-long broomstick with a saw, sanding the rough edges.

To make your broom even more special, find a small stuffed animal that you don't mind cutting a bit. Snip a hole in the top and the bottom of the back of the toy, and work a hole through the stuffing with a screwdriver. Slip your stuffed pet over the handle of the broom and push it down low on the broomstick. Now you both are ready to sweep!

Start in one corner of a room, and sweep all the way across the end of the room. Sweep with low, easy swings, so the dirt you are sweeping up doesn't fly through the air. When you get to the end of the room, step back several feet into the room and sweep your way back across. Your mother will love to have your help keeping the house clean!

Jesus Understood

LITTLE Armando was crossing a busy city street when a big car came around a corner and knocked him down. He was badly hurt, and some kind people hurried him away to a hospital. Poor Armando was in great pain, and the doctors and nurses were afraid he would die.

In the hospital Armando found himself in the same room with a little boy named Chico. The two quickly became friends. Chico knew something about Jesus, but Armando knew almost nothing at all about Him.

Chico said, "You know, Armando, I've heard that someday, after we are dead, Jesus will come and wake us up, and take us to heaven where there are plenty of good things to eat, and everybody is happy. You just have to ask Him, and He'll take you there."

"But I couldn't ask Somebody so big and important like that,"

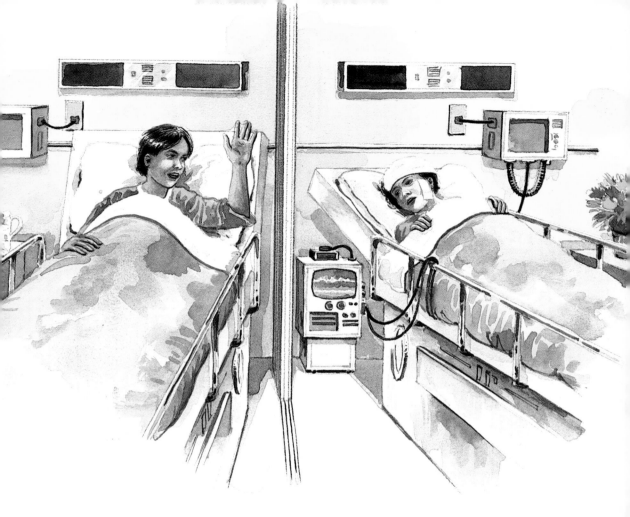

Armando said. "He wouldn't listen to a little boy like me."

"Oh, yes, He would," Chico said, "but you don't have to ask Him. Just put up your hand—like we do in school—when He comes through the hospital. They say He comes through every evening when the lights are turned out."

Evening came. Nurse went around the ward and turned out some of the lights.

"I think it's nearly time," said Chico. "Put up your hand, Armando."

79

Armando tried, but he was so weak he couldn't. Every time he put his hand up, it fell down.

Chico crept out of bed, and with a pillow, he managed to prop up Armando's hand so that it wouldn't fall down.

"Thank you, Chico," murmured Armando. "Do you think Jesus will see it?"

"I'm sure He will," said Chico.

In the morning the little hand was still there. Armando was dead, but Jesus had understood.

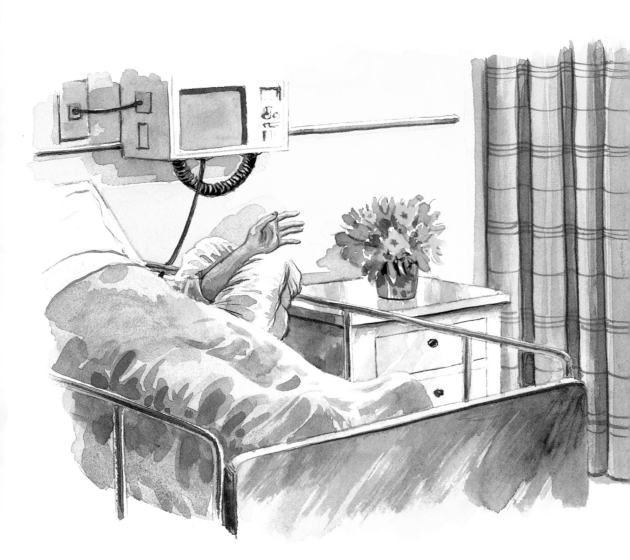

Story Theme—**Health Habits**

Poor Dalia

"OH DEAR!" cried Layla, wringing her hands, "what's the matter with Dalia? I must get the doctor at once."

Laying poor Dalia down on her pretty white bed, Layla picked up her toy telephone and pretended to call her family doctor. "Hello! Is that you, Dr. Pills?"

"Yes, madam," came a voice from the other side of the door. "This is Dr. Pills. What can I do for you?"

"Oh, Doctor, my poor Dalia is sick. Please come quickly."

"I'll be right there," said the voice in the hall. "My car is waiting outside, so it'll just take me a minute."

Layla went back to Dalia's bedside and tried hard to cry over her. There was a knock at the door, and she opened it.

"Ah, here you are, Dr. Pills. I'm so glad you've come."

Dr. Pills, wearing Dad's best hat and carrying his briefcase, walked

over to the bed. He tried to look serious as he took off his gloves.

"Let me feel her pulse," he said, taking Dalia's tiny hand.

"Ah, very fast, very fast," he murmured.

"Poor Dalia!" said Layla.

"Now let me look at her tongue," said Dr. Pills.

"I'm afraid she's too sick to open her mouth," said Layla. "Please tell me what you think is wrong."

"A serious case," said Dr. Pills. "Very serious."

"Oh, what shall I do, what shall I do?" cried Layla, wringing her hands.

"Do?" said Dr. Pills. "There is only one thing to do. You must treat the child better. You have been feeding her wrong. She has acute indigestion, and probably will die."

"Die! Oh dear, how terrible!" exclaimed Layla. "What should I

feed her to make her well and strong again?"

"Ahem!" said Dr. Pills. "Let me see. This child has been eating too much candy. She has been eating it all day long, and it has ruined her stomach. You must stop giving her candy except at meals."

"But she will cry!" said Layla.

"Never mind," said Dr. Pills. "Better cry than die. Children must not eat between meals. It is very bad for them. And, let me see, does she eat plenty of green leafy vegetables?"

"Oh, no, Doctor. She hates greens. Whenever I put them on the table she grumbles terribly."

"Never mind," said Dr. Pills sternly. "Better grumble than be ill. She must eat something green every day—lettuce, cabbage, sprouts, broccoli, and things like that."

"Not all of them every day!"

"Of course not!" said Dr. Pills. "But at least one of them every day. And let me see, does the child get enough fruit?"

"She likes bananas and pears, but they are so expensive I can't afford to give her very many."

"She must have plenty of fruit. Stop giving her sugary cakes and pastries, and give her apples and oranges instead."

"I once heard," said Layla, "that an apple a day keeps the doctor away. Is that true?"

"Certainly," said Dr. Pills. "I'll *never* have to come back again if you do—unless, of course, she catches pneumonia or something like that."

"Oh, thank you so much, Dr. Pills," said Layla. "How much do you charge?"

"My fee is $25," said Dr. Pills.

"Rather high, isn't it?" said Layla, taking two big buttons and five little buttons out of her purse.

"My usual charge," said Dr. Pills. "Thank you. I'm sure your daughter will be better soon. And be sure you follow my instructions."

"I will," said Layla as she closed the door. "But, Aren," she called, "you won't forget to put Daddy's hat back in the proper place, will you?"

Sprouts to Eat

Sprouts are good for you, and fun to make. Use a canning jar, the screw-on ring of a canning lid, and a piece of hardware cloth (plastic window screen) cut to fit the top of the jar. Put two or three tablespoons of seeds such as lentils, alfalfa seeds, pinto beans, or kidney beans in the bottom of the jar. Cover the jar with the screen and screw on the lid.

Let the bigger seeds soak overnight. Pour water through the screen, and rinse the seeds. Be sure to let the water drain back out of the jar. Rinse the seeds each day. In a few days you will begin to see the seeds sprout.

If you let the sprouts grow in the light, they will be greener than if they grow in the dark. Alfalfa sprouts are good in salads or sandwiches. The other, larger seeds are good cooked and spread on toast, or with other chop suey vegetables.

Love Unlimited

I WAS in Australia, traveling by car from Newcastle to Sydney. It had been a very busy day and I was tired. I slouched down on the front seat beside the driver, hoping to get a little sleep on the way home.

Then I heard it—the voice of a little girl talking very sadly to her mother. "Well, I love him anyway," she said.

Instantly I was alert. Sitting behind me in the back seat was 6-year-old Suzanne looking at her mother and talking earnestly about something very important.

"What was that you said?" I asked.

"I love him anyway," said Suzanne, with tears in her voice.

"Whom do you love so much?" I asked.

"My dog," said Suzanne.

"But doesn't everybody love your dog?"

"No," said Suzanne. "My mamma doesn't."

"What sort of dog is it?" I asked. "Is it a very big one?"

"No," said Suzanne. "It's just a teeny-weeny pug puppy."

"And your mother doesn't love it?"

"No," said Suzanne. "And she wants to get rid of it."

"But why doesn't your mother love your dog?" I asked.

"Because he chewed up her new shoes and tore up some of her clothes."

"Oh, that was bad of him," I said. "What else did he do?"

"He pulled a sheet off the clothesline. And he tore up a newspaper and left the pieces all over the garage."

"Anything else?"

"Oh, yes. When Mother takes the trash outside he brings it right

back. The other day he brought a whole lot of melon rinds and piled them on the kitchen floor."

"I can see why Mother doesn't love him very much," I said. "How about Daddy? Does he love the puppy?"

"He doesn't love him either."

"Why not?"

"Well, you see, just after Daddy washed and polished his car the other day, my dog ran all over it with his muddy feet. And was Daddy angry!"

"I can understand that," I said. "You must have quite a lively little dog."

"Oh, he's bad," said Suzanne. "I know he's bad. And Mamma doesn't love him and Daddy doesn't love him and nobody loves him—"

"Except you," I broke in.

"'Cept me," said Suzanne. "I love him anyway."

Suddenly I thought of all the boys and girls in the world who are just like Suzanne's little dog. Lively, mischievous, and naughty as can be—but their mothers love them anyway.

Isn't that the way your mother loves you? No matter what you do, no matter how bad you get sometimes, she still loves you, and will go on loving you as long as you live.

And that's how it is with Daddy, too.

God is like that. He never stops loving us despite all our mistakes. He never gives up hoping that we will be good. The Bible speaks of the length and breadth and height and depth of the love of God, and says it is beyond our understanding. It is. It is just too big. It is "as far as the east is from the west" and you could never measure that, could you?

God's love is without limit and without end.

Somehow little Suzanne felt the greatness of His love when she said, talking about her naughty dog, "I love him anyway."

Story Theme—**Confession; Courage; Responsibility**

Seventeen Cowards

BILL came rushing into the house and flopped breathlessly down in a chair. He looked scared.

At that moment Dad came in from work. "What's the matter, Bill?" he asked anxiously.

"Oh, nothing," said Bill.

"Yes there is," said Dad. "I can tell by the look on your face. What's happened?"

"Oh, well, Dad," said Bill, wriggling uncomfortably, "you see, we were all playing ball up there on that vacant lot near Mrs. Boliger's. You know where it is, Dad, about half a mile from here."

"Yes, I know all about it," said Dad. "I used to play on it myself when I was a boy."

"Well, the ball—" hesitated Bill.

"I know what you are going to say," said Dad. "The ball went

91

through Mrs. Boliger's window."

"Well, yes, Dad. That's what happened. It was an accident, but how did you know?"

"I just guessed," said Dad. "But why are you so scared?"

"I'm not really scared," said Bill, "but, you know, Mrs. Boliger is such a mean old woman. She makes such a fuss about things like that."

"What did you all do after the window was broken?"

"We ran away."

92

"You ran away!"

"Yes."

"How many boys were playing?"

"Seventeen."

"All 17 of you ran away, afraid of what some elderly woman might say to you?"

"Yes, Dad," said Bill, hanging his head a little.

"Well," said Dad, "it sounds like 17 cowards were playing ball."

Bill didn't like that, but he knew the charge was true. For a moment he tried to defend himself.

"But Dad, Mrs. Boliger is such an old crab!" he said.

"Maybe she is," Dad said. "But if you boys broke her window, don't you think you should have had the courage to go and tell her you did it and offer to pay for it? It wouldn't have cost you more than a few dollars each. By the way, who hit the ball that broke the window?"

Bill hesitated. "I did," he said dejectedly.

"I thought so," said Dad. "What are you going to do about it?" The two of them stared out the window for a few minutes.

"I suppose I should go talk to her," Bill said finally. "But I can't! I just can't! She's such a mean old thing."

"But I think it would be the right thing to do. Get yourself cleaned up, and we'll go."

"You mean you're going with me?"

"Yes, I'll go with you as far as Mrs. Boliger's front gate, and then you can go on to the door and speak to her by yourself."

"Oh, brother!" Bill muttered to himself as he got off his chair and went to the bathroom to wash his hands and brush his hair. Eventually he came downstairs again, where Dad was all ready, waiting for him. Together they set out for Mrs. Boliger's.

Bill couldn't have been more scared if he had been on his way to prison. "Do I really have to go?" he asked after a while.

"I'm afraid there's no other way," said Dad. "And you'll feel much happier when you've done the right thing."

Silence fell again. They walked on, Bill wishing that Mrs. Boliger's house was 20 miles away, so Dad would get tired and give up.

At last they turned a corner and came to the vacant lot where the accident had taken place. Mrs. Boliger's house was in full view, and so was the broken window.

"Here we are," said Father, as they reached the little white gate at the entrance to Mrs. Boliger's property. "I'll wait here while you go to the house and speak to her. I'll be nearby if you need me."

Bill had to go on alone. He felt sure that Mrs. Boliger's eyes were watching him as he walked all the way up the sidewalk, and he kept thinking to himself, *What will she say when I tell her I was the one who broke her window?*

94

Bill rang the bell. It sounded loud and long, like a tolling bell of doom. The door opened, and there stood Mrs. Boliger. To Bill's surprise she was smiling. He hadn't expected that.

"How are you?" she said kindly. "What can I do for you?"

"Well—er—well—er," stuttered Bill, blushing all over, "I—er—I—er—am the boy who—er—hit the ball that—er—broke your window this afternoon, and I'm—I'm sorry."

Bill hesitated and turned away a little as if he was waiting for a bomb to explode.

But it didn't. Instead he heard a sweet voice saying, "I am proud of you, son. I have had my windows broken this way many, many times, but you are the first boy who has ever come to tell me about it. You are a real gentleman and surely were brought up well. You must have a wonderful father."

"Oh," said Bill, "that's my dad over there. He happened to come along with me."

At this, of course, Dad had to come up the path and join them.

"You have a fine boy here," said Mrs. Boliger. "In fact, I think he's the grandest boy I've ever met. You know, sir, no boy has ever come here before and spoken to me like this about breaking my windows."

"Well, Mrs. Boliger," said Dad, "Bill and I would like to pay you for putting the glass in again."

"Oh, dear," said Mrs. Boliger. "I'd hate to make you pay when the others never have. I think I have a piece of glass."

Bill beamed.

"Then Bill and I will put it in for you," said Dad.

They all talked together while the glass was put in place. Then Dad and Bill said goodbye and started for home.

"I suppose," said Dad, "you aren't sorry you went to see her?"

"I should say not," said Bill. "Why, she was as nice as pie. I never would have dreamed that Mrs. Boliger could be like that. I

wonder why the boys say that she is mean. She isn't a bit mean. She couldn't have been kinder or more considerate."

"Boys say those things sometimes because they don't understand," said Dad. "By the way, Bill, don't you feel better now since you have done the right thing, the brave thing?"

"Do I!" said Bill. "I could jump clear over the moon!"

Baseball History

Baseball developed from a game milkmaids and farmhands played with an upside-down three-legged stool during the 1300s. The batter tried to hit the ball before the ball hit the stool. The players used other stools for bases.

Stoolball was such fun that Governor Bradford, in charge of one of America's first colonies, complained that some boys even wanted to play it on Christmas Day! The game changed over the years, until in 1744 an English publication described the popular new game baseball for the first time.

When the Well Dried Up

RENE was so thirsty. There was very little water anywhere, since it hadn't rained for many, many days. Not a cloud had crossed the sky, and the fierce African sun had scorched the land for hundreds of square miles. The rivers and streams had dried up, and now the deep well close to the farmhouse had run dry.

Rene's daddy didn't know what to do. He had worked very hard

for many years to build up that home and to develop his land. Now it seemed that he was about to lose everything. His crops were withering away, and worse still, his cattle were parched with thirst, for there was no water to give them. What could he do?

Calling his family together, he told them how serious the situation was and that he was going to ask Jesus to send rain. They all knelt down—Mother, Daddy, Rene, and her baby sister—and together they prayed as they had never prayed before. Father and Mother both prayed very earnestly that Jesus somehow would send rain to save the crops and to spare the herds of cattle.

When it was Rene's turn to pray, however, she asked for something different. She said, "Dear Jesus, if You don't send rain, please send some water into the well."

Daddy smiled, because he couldn't see how water could come into the well if it didn't rain. But Rene didn't think about that. She believed that Jesus could do anything. And when they all got

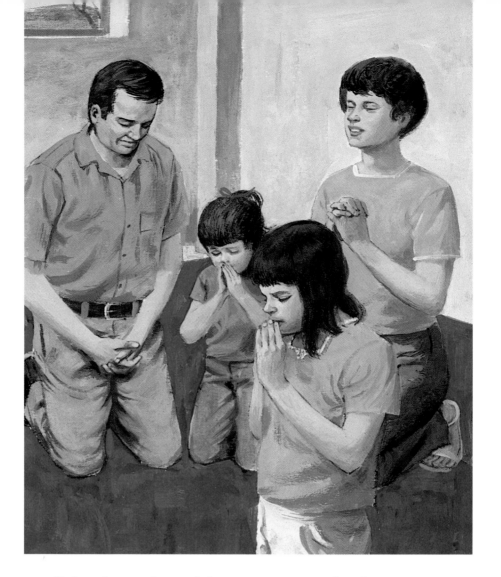

up off their knees she said she was quite sure that Jesus was going
to answer her prayer.

Father and Mother went about their various tasks around the
home, but Rene disappeared. She had gone to the well to watch
what Jesus would do.

She pulled and pushed at the cover, and finally succeeded in
moving it enough so that she could look down. But the well was so

deep and dark that she couldn't see anything. Picking up a stone, she dropped it in and listened intently. There was a moment of breathless waiting. Then "Splash!"

The next instant she was off to the house as fast as her legs could run.

"Jesus has sent the water!" she cried. "Jesus has sent the water!"

Father wouldn't believe it. He came running to the well to see, with Mother and the farm workers close behind. He dropped in another pebble, and there was another splash. A moment later he had the pump working, and soon a stream of clear, cold water poured out of the well.

How happy and thankful they all were! And do you know, from that day to this, that well has never run dry. Of course, some people say, "It just happened that way." But Rene knows better. She says Jesus sent the water in the well and answered a little girl's prayer, and I believe she is right.

Penny's Extra Present

IT WAS a week before Christmas. Eight-year-old Penny and her little brother Marcus were shopping with Mother.

They were having such a happy time! It was great fun buying presents for everybody and spending all the money they had been saving up for the past few months.

Penny's arms were full of packages. She had a present for Daddy, another for Marcus, and a very special one for Mother. Oh, yes, and still another for Aunt Jane and a teeny-weeny one for cousin Mary, who was only 6 months old.

Mother had a lot of packages too, and she was standing at a counter in the toy department buying one more present when the worst thing possible happened. Marcus disappeared!

Penny was the first to notice he had gone. "Mother!" she called. "Where's Marcus?"

102

Mother looked around anxiously. "Marcus?" she said. "Isn't he with you?"

"No. He just ran away. How can we ever find him in this crowd of people?"

"Oh dear!" cried Mother. "I can't leave this counter, because I'm in the middle of paying a bill. Will you go and look for him?"

"But I'll drop my packages," said Penny.

"Put them down here and I'll look after them."

Hastily Penny put her armful of packages on a stack of books and hurried off to search for her little brother.

"Marcus! Marcus!" she shouted as she dodged between and around the shoppers as they stood in the aisles and crowded around the counters.

She felt pretty sure that Marcus was still somewhere in the toy department, probably looking at something that had caught his attention earlier in the afternoon.

She was right. Turning a corner, she saw him sitting in a "space-ship." He was perfectly happy and hadn't even thought that perhaps his mother and big sister were wondering where he was.

"Marcus!" cried Penny. "You shouldn't run away like this. Mother is terribly worried about you." Taking him firmly by the hand, she hurried back to Mother.

"Here he is," she said. "Now where did I leave my packages?"

"Over there," said Mother, "on that pile of books. Pick them up and we'll go home before Marcus gets into more mischief."

Penny gathered up her packages, tucked them as carefully as she could under her arm, and followed Mother and Marcus to the door and onto the bus and home.

"Look!" Penny exclaimed as she sorted out her things on the kitchen table. "I've got an extra present!"

"What do you mean?" asked Mother.

"See what I have!" she cried, holding up a beautiful book of animal pictures.

"Did you buy that?" asked Mother.

"Oh, no," said Penny. "I never saw it before."

"Then where did you get it?"

"I don't know. I just found it on the table."

"Penny," said Mother seriously, "you must have picked that up in the shop by mistake."

"Maybe I did," said Penny.

Mother looked at the book. "It's lovely," she said. "And see the price—$25.95!"

"Just think, I brought home a book like that without knowing it!" said Penny. "I hope nobody will think I stole it!"

"What do you think we should do about it?" asked Mother.

"Oh," said Penny right away, "I'm sure Jesus would want me to send it back, wouldn't He?"

"Yes," said Mother. "And I'm glad you thought of that first. It would be nice if you would write a little note to the manager, telling him how it happened. Then we'll wrap the book up carefully and send it back."

"Maybe I should write the letter now while I'm thinking about it," said Penny.

"A good idea," said Mother. "And I'll get supper ready."

So Penny wrote a little note. It said:

"Dear Mr. Manager: This afternoon when I was in your shop I accidentally picked up a book with my other packages. I didn't find out about it until I got home. I'm very sorry. And because I didn't pay for it I'm sure Jesus would want me to send it back. So I'm sending it. From your friend, Penny."

Mother read the note and said she thought it was very nice. Then she tucked it into the book and packaged it for mailing.

A few days later, just before Christmas, Penny received a reply to her letter. The manager wrote to say how pleased he was to know that there was such an honest girl in town. And because she had sent the book back so promptly, he was sending her a little present to show his appreciation.

When the gift arrived, it turned out to be a pair of beautiful red slippers. They were so lovely and so unexpected that Penny could hardly believe her eyes. She put them on and danced all around the house in pure delight. Every time she wore those slippers, she felt a warm glow inside. She was so glad that she had done the right thing and sent that book back!

Honesty

How would you describe an honest person? First, make a list of what an honest person does do, then make a list of what an honest person doesn't do. You will probably include in your first list that an honest person tells the truth. In your second list, you might mention that he or she doesn't lie or steal. What else is on your list?

Would you like your friends to be honest? Why? Do you try to be honest with your friends?

Sometimes being honest takes extra time and trouble, but it's worth it, as Penny found out in the story.

The Secret of Happiness

THE RADIO weather report said that snow was coming. This was good news for Joe and Gerald. It set them ablaze with energy.

They had often talked about making sleds for themselves, but they had never gotten around to doing it. The good news about the snow made them decide that now was the time, and they eagerly began to work.

Every moment they could spare from their schoolwork the boys spent in the shed in Gerald's backyard sawing, planing, hammering, until at last the sleds were finished and ready for the snow to fall.

But it didn't come. Maybe the clouds blew away after the weather experts had looked at them. However it happened, for many days there were two sleds in the shed with nothing to slide them on.

108

School closed for Christmas, and still there was no snow. Day
after day went by, cold and wet. There seemed about as much
prospect of snow as of a heat wave. The boys gave up hope and
wished they had never taken the trouble to make their sleds.

At last Christmas Eve arrived and with it came a sudden change.
The rain stopped, the thermometer dropped with a rush, and a
strong wind came up.

"Something is going to happen," said Joe, as he went to bed that
night. And he was right.

In the morning the clouds had gone, and the rising sun glistened
on a vast expanse of snow. A heavy snowfall had covered the whole
landscape with a glorious white mantle—just what the boys were
hoping for.

Gerald was delighted. As soon as he woke up he guessed what

had happened, for he could see the reflection of the snow on the ceiling. He leaped out of bed, dressed as quickly as he could, and rushed out to the shed where the precious sleds had been stored so long. He hauled them both over the snow up to the house and then ran off to find Joe.

How happy they were! This was better than their highest expectations. No Christmas Day could have started out better. They decided that they would head out right away to a neighboring hill and have all the fun they had been dreaming about.

They trotted down the street dragging their sleds behind them. School friends shouted to them, all eager to share in the fun.

"Lucky guys!" they cried. "Can we have a ride on your sled?"

"Not now," answered Joe and Gerald. "We're going off by ourselves today."

"Lend us one of your sleds," called another.

"Nothing doing!" shouted Joe. "You should have made one for yourself."

Ralph Morton, the lame boy, waved his hand cheerfully from his window, and wished them lots of fun.

"Nice of him, wasn't it?" said Gerald.

"Yes," said Joe, " 'specially since he can never hope to pilot a
sled of his own."

Just then they passed Sara Halley's house. They had always been
friendly with her and her little sisters. She greeted them cheerfully
as usual and wished them a happy Christmas.

"Wish I could come for a slide," she said, "but I can't today.
I'm helping Mother all I can, so that she can have a really
happy Christmas."

The boys hurried on. Soon they were out of the town and climb-
ing the hill, dragging their sleds behind them. Then they prepared
their slide and the fun began.

Swish! Away they went down the hill. Then up to the top again.

Then another glorious slide. They played together for a couple of hours.

After a while, however, Joe noticed a change coming over Gerald's face. "What's up, Gerald?" asked Joe as they climbed the hill together, this time a bit more slowly.

"Nothing much," said Gerald, "only somehow I'm not getting as much fun out of this as I thought I would."

"Aren't you?" said Joe. "I'm not, either. Of course, it's nice in a way, but I don't feel comfortable. I wonder why."

"Funny we both feel the same way, isn't it?" said Gerald.

"Very funny," said Joe, as they trudged on up to the top.

112

Swish! Down they went again.

On the way up the next time they talked about their strange feelings again.

"I think I know what's the matter," said Joe.

"What?" asked Gerald.

"I keep thinking about Ralph."

"So do I," said Gerald. "And Sara and the others. I wish we hadn't left them behind. Mean of us, wasn't it?"

"Yes," said Joe.

There was silence again as they climbed slowly upward.

"Let's just have one more," said Joe.

"All right," said Gerald.

They had the last slide, and then turned toward home. On the way they talked of how they would spend the afternoon. As they reached the town they stopped at the homes of some of their friends who had no sleds. What Gerald and Joe said to them seemed to make them very happy.

Dinner was scarcely over when there was a loud knock at their front door. Running out, Joe and Gerald found a happy, excited group of children waiting for them.

"Hurrah!" they all cried when they saw the two boys. "I'll be first," said one, and "Me, me, me, first!" called another.

Then sorting the visitors out, Joe and Gerald put two or three of them on each sled and took them for rides up and down the street. Oh, the shrieks of joy and laughter that could be heard!

All afternoon they kept it up—except for a game of snowball now and then. All the children took turns riding until at last, too tired to run anymore, Joe and Gerald sent them all home and put the hard-worked sleds back in the shed.

Kami's Slippers

KATELYN wasn't in a very good mood. She was grizzling—if you know what that means. It's sort of halfway between a cry and a whine. Little girls get the complaint every now and then, usually when they want what they can't get or when they don't like what they do get.

Katelyn's grizzling this time was about a paintbox. You see, Katelyn had a paintbox and her sister Kami had a paintbox. Kami had used up all the paint in her box. She liked to pour lots of water into her paint and paint big pictures on Daddy's newspapers, so her paint hadn't lasted long.

Kami began to look longingly at Katelyn's paintbox. But Katelyn, since she had painted smaller pictures than Kami and still had some paint left, thought it wasn't fair that she had to share her paint with Kami.

115

The two girls had a strong difference of opinion about the problem. Kami made a grab at Katelyn's paintbox, and Katelyn defended her box by jabbing Kami in the nose with her paintbrush. It was a very unhappy quarrel, and it might have become much worse if Mother hadn't suddenly appeared and marched both girls outside to cool off.

But Katelyn didn't forget her troubles, and grizzled all the time about what Kami had done or tried to do. She told Kami that she would never let her have any of her paint, never.

At last they were called in to supper. And then something else went wrong. They had to take off their outdoor shoes and put on their slippers when they came into the house, but Katelyn discovered that her slippers were missing. She looked high and low, but they were gone.

By this time Kami had her slippers on, which only made Katelyn more desperate. "Huh, huh, huh," she began to grizzle again, "I can't find my slippers. Huh, huh, huh!"

Once more she looked in every corner she could think of, wandering around in her socks crying, "Huh, huh, huh, somebody's got my slippers."

And then a beautiful thing happened. As Katelyn came into the dining room crying "Huh, huh, huh," Kami took off one of her slippers. "Here you are, Katelyn," she said, "we'll each have one."

Katelyn's face lighted up with a smile as she eagerly seized the slipper and put it on her left foot. Then, hand in hand, they went off together to hunt for Katelyn's slippers. How funny it was to hear them wandering around the house—*clod, thump, clod, thump, clod, thump—each with one foot in a slipper*.

Suddenly there was a cry of joy. Katelyn's slippers were found—in their usual place, of course, under her bed! Happily they came downstairs together, hands clasped and faces radiant.

After supper they were allowed to stay up a little while, since Mother wanted to finish the ironing before putting them to bed. So they began painting Daddy's newspaper again, and two brushes dipped vigorously and with perfect peace and harmony into Katelyn's paintbox.

Kami's happy little thought had driven all the grizzles away.

Tinker— The Tale of a Puppy

DADDY! Come see what we've found in the yard!"

Larry and Rosa dragged Daddy out of the study and into the kitchen, where the oddest, prettiest little pup was wriggling and frisking about.

"Please let us keep him," pleaded Larry. "He's just a poor little stray thing, and he needs a home."

"But I have two puppies already," said Daddy, looking at Larry and Rosa, "and I can't afford to keep any more."

"Oh, just this one baby thing," pleaded Rosa. "I'm sure he won't cost much to keep."

"Perhaps he belongs to someone," said Daddy, who didn't want the puppy at all.

"Oh, no, we've asked everybody around, and they don't know where he came from."

119

"Well, you can keep him for a little while," said Daddy.

What joy! They could keep him! He was to be their very own!

Just then the puppy collided with the milk carton Rosa had left on the floor beside a saucer. A moment later a white stream was flowing across the floor, and the puppy was licking up the mess as rapidly as his little tongue could manage.

"You bad dog!" cried Larry. "But I am sure he'll never do it again."

"We'll have to get a good name for him," said Rosa. "Let's call him Tinker." So Tinker he was.

Weeks passed, during which the children became more and more fond of their pet. Tinker grew rapidly, and was soon almost as much a part of the family as the children themselves, although Daddy never seemed quite pleased with having a stray dog in the family circle.

One night, Tinker had been put in the workshop to sleep as usual. Long after everyone had gone to bed, Tinker woke up. Something was wrong. There was a strange choking smell coming out of the kitchen. Tinker thought he had better call his master, in case something was wrong.

120

"Yap! Yap! Yap!"

No answer.

The smoke grew more dense, and Tinker barked again. "Yap! Yap! Yap!"

Mr. Norman woke up. "There's that dog barking. Why does he want to wake us up in the middle of the night? I wish I'd never allowed him in the place."

"Yap! Yap! Yap!"

Mr. Norman got out of bed. "Well," he said, "I smell burning wood."

In an instant he was downstairs and found the kitchen on fire and full of smoke. Running to the faucet, he threw bucket after bucket of water on the flames and put out the fire. He had come just in time. In a few more minutes, the fire would have been out of control.

In the morning Daddy gave Tinker a breakfast more wonderful than he had ever imagined in his wildest puppy dreams. Larry and Rosa couldn't love him enough. Daddy went so far as to say that without Tinker they might have lost their home and even their lives.

From that day on, he always said Tinker was the most wonderful dog he had ever known, and Mother said, "What if we hadn't let Tinker stay!"

Fire Plan

Pretend you are a firefighter, and check your house for fire safety precautions. You can make a firefighter's hat by cutting a long rectangle out of heavy paper (like a grocery sack) about 14 inches by 9 inches. Cut off the front corners in an oval shape and lightly round off the back corners. Cut half an oval big enough for the top of your head to fit into.

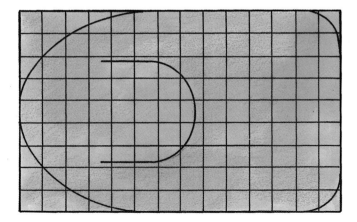

As you make the rounds of your house, ask yourself these questions. Do you know where the fire extinguisher is? How do you use it? Do you know how to open the windows and remove any screens so you can get out easily? Are there stickers on the windows that indicate rooms where the very young or very old people are sleeping, so firefighters can give special attention to these rooms in an emergency? Does your family have plans for exiting the house when there is a fire? Why not ask your parents to help you make a safety plan?

Dennis and the Dive Bombers

IT LOOKED as if all the boys in the neighborhood were going off to war. Dennis stood at the gate of his home and watched wide-eyed as they hurried by. Some of them carried wooden guns over their shoulders, some had wooden swords, and others had pointed sticks that were supposed to be spears.

"Where are you going?" he called to some of the boys he knew.

"Come on!" they cried excitedly. "We're going to fight the enemy."

"Who's the enemy?" asked Dennis.

"We've found a wasps' nest out in the woods, and we're all going out to beat 'em up."

"Mom!" Dennis cried as he ran indoors. "May I go to war with all the other boys?"

"What kind of war?" asked
Mother.

"They're all going out to the
woods to fight the wasps, and
they all have swords and guns and
things. Let me go too—
please, Mom."

Just then Daddy came in the
house and asked what was going
on. When he heard about the boys
going to war, he shook his head.

"It's a very foolish thing to do," he said. "Wasps can be very dangerous enemies, and you must be properly prepared to fight them. You can't hope to win against wasps with pieces of wood."

So Dennis had to content himself with standing at the gate waiting for the boys to come back. After what seemed an age, the boys came rushing past, waving their weapons in the air and shouting about their great victory, although just what they had done to the wasps he never did find out.

Two days later he saw the boys going by the house again, just as they had done before, each one with his "weapon" of war.

"Come on, Dennis," they cried. "Don't be a sissy!"

"Dad doesn't think it's a good idea," he said.

"Oh, come on," they called; "he won't mind. It's going to be great fun."

Dennis wavered. He could go with the boys and get back with-

out Daddy knowing anything about it, since he was away at his office and wouldn't be back for hours. Mom was out too. It would be such fun to go with the others, and he did want to find out how they fought wasps with wooden swords and spears.

Picking up a piece of wood to make a weapon for himself, he marched out to the battle.

When they reached the woods, some of the bigger boys began searching around for a wasps' nest. It wasn't long before one of them called, "I have one. Here it is. And my, aren't they big fellows!"

They *were* big fellows. They weren't wasps at all—they were hornets, and before long *they* were going into battle, while the boys were running pell-mell in every direction.

One of the hornets landed on poor Dennis, stinging him on his upper lip just under his nose. In a few moments his lip swelled up into a huge lump.

He was in terrible pain, and hardly knew how he got home. How he wished he had listened to his daddy's advice! What would he say?

When Mom saw what had happened, she was so frightened that she took him to the doctor for treatment. Dennis suffered so much that Daddy didn't even say "I told you so."

But one day when Dennis was almost better Daddy said, "Well, Dennis, it doesn't sound like the boys won that battle they went out to fight."

"No," said Dennis. "The enemy had too many dive bombers. We couldn't do a thing."

"I can think of another reason," said Daddy.

"What?" asked Dennis.

"You were picking a fight with creatures that just want to be left alone so they can go about their business. Wasps and hornets have a place in our world like every other creature God made."

"I can't think of any place hornets ought to have," Dennis said, wincing as he thought of the terrible pain he had been through.

"Well, they do," Daddy said. "Did you know that many of them lay their eggs in larvae which keeps them from developing into insect pests? They do us a good service. And unless they decide to live too close to our homes where we might accidently bother them into attacking us, I think we ought to leave them pretty much alone. Don't you?"

"I sure do," Dennis said.

Tom's Thought-lessness

SCHOOL was closed for the afternoon and Tom was spending the free time with some of his friends in the park. They all had brought their lunch, and after playing tag and many other games, they sat down under a fine old oak tree to enjoy the good things their mothers had packed for them.

Soon they had finished, and since they didn't have anything better to do, they began throwing the banana skins and orange peels at one another and scattering their lunch wrappings all over the place.

They were too busy to notice an elderly gentleman coming toward them from behind the oak tree. He was going to walk past the boys, but stepping on one of the banana skins, he fell heavily to the ground.

Tom sprang to his side and did his best to help him to his feet again. "I hope you're not hurt, sir," he said.

"I think not," said the gentleman. "Just a little shaken. I think

130

I will sit on the bench for a little while if I may. I must rest a
few minutes."

Tom helped him across to the bench, and the boys stood around
to see whether the gentleman had hurt himself. The man sat down
carefully on the bench.

"I think I'm all right," he said, "but I'm getting old now, and a
fall like that is dangerous for one of my age. It's too bad that people
are so careless with their banana skins, isn't it?"

"Yes," said Tom, with a guilty look at the other boys.

"I hope you boys never throw banana skins around."

"Um," said Tom, blushing a little.

"So selfish, isn't it?" went on the elderly gentleman.

"I suppose it is," said Tom.

"If people only thought of the pain they might cause others, I'm sure they would never do it."

"No," said Tom.

"And look at all that paper lying around," said the elderly gentleman. "Some lazy, thoughtless people must have been here recently."

"Yes," said Tom, for there was really nothing else he could say.

"If only," went on the gentleman, "if only people would stop to think about others, they would never leave a mess like this behind them, would they?"

"No," said Tom, getting more uncomfortable.

"You know," said the gentleman, "this is a beautiful park. But if everyone left a mess like this, it wouldn't be worth coming to. If it were all covered with dirty paper and orange peels and banana skins you boys wouldn't want to play here, would you?"

"No, sir," said Tom and the other boys together.

"Well, boys, I'm feeling better now. Thank you for helping me up. I'll be off again, I think. Here's something for you, son, to get some candy."

To Tom's amazement, he handed him a dollar and walked away.

The boys looked at one another.

"I thought he was going to scold us," said one.

"He didn't see us," said another.

"Don't you believe it," said Tom. "I think he saw everything we did."

"Anyhow, he was a good sport," said a third.

132

"And I liked what he said," said Tom. "He was very kind about it."

"You're right," said another. "And that's the last time I'm going to throw stuff around here."

"I feel the same way," said Tom, and he began to pick up some of the litter he had so carelessly scattered a little while before. Strangely enough, the other boys got the same idea. They didn't say much while they were doing it, but within a few minutes all the banana skins, orange peels, and lunch wrappers had been picked up and dropped into one of the park trash cans.

"Well," said Tom, as he led the others off to spend the dollar, "I don't think we'll litter up this place again."

"No, we won't!" chorused the others.

And sure enough, they didn't.

Thoughtful Treasure Hunt

When your mother isn't around, make a treasure hunt for her in the kitchen. Hide little surprises in unexpected places. You can put a pretty picture of a flower with a poem about flowers on it in the container of flour on the counter. Hide a coupon somewhere on the fridge for "One Refrigerator Cleaned Upon Request" by you, of course. Fold up a paper with a Bible verse about honey, and tape it to the honey jar.

You can make treasure hunts for other members of your family, too. Wrap a small present and hide it under a brother's or sister's pillow. Write coupons good for several car washes to be performed by yourself, and hide them in your dad's sock drawer. You can think of many more ideas that will keep your family smiling at unexpected times, in unexpected places.

How Toby Made Peace

NOW LOOK here, kids," said Daddy, sending Paul and Barbara out of the living room into the yard. "I can't stand it anymore. You stay outside until you can learn to stop grumbling and be more polite to each other."

And with that Daddy went back into the living room, leaned back in his easy chair, and went to sleep.

Paul and Barbara knew they deserved being sent outside, and they were sorry they had annoyed Daddy so much. For a little while they didn't know what to do, and wandered aimlessly up and down the backyard in silence.

"Ah, here's Toby coming!" cried Paul. "Toby, Toby, Toby! Good old Toby, where have you been?"

Toby wagged his tail, as if to assure them that he had been a very good dog all the time he had been missing.

135

"And you haven't been chasing any cats?" asked Barbara. Toby yawned and wagged his tail again, as if to say that he wouldn't think of doing anything like that. Although, if the truth must be told, nothing stirred Toby's wrath as much as the sight of a kitty's whiskers.

"I've got an idea," said Paul.

"Tell me," said Barbara.

"Let's give Toby a bath. He hasn't had one for a long time, and he's getting dirty."

"I think that would be fun," said Barbara. "It's better than doing nothing. You get the tub out of the shed, and I'll slip into the kitchen quietly and see if I can find a towel and some soap."

"Right!" cried Paul. "Won't that be nice, Toby? Toby have a bath? Dear old Toby!"

Again Toby wagged his tail, though it was not quite so happy a wag as before. He didn't like having a bath, and sometimes objected to it very strongly. He looked suspiciously at the tub as Paul brought it out of the shed, and decided it was about time he took a short walk.

Barbara soon returned, bringing a towel and a kettle of warm water. "Where's Toby?" she asked.

"Ran off," said Paul. "We'll have to catch him."

"Toby, Toby!" called Barbara.

But Toby was a wise old dog and guessed why he was wanted. He walked a little farther on. Paul and Barbara followed him, and after an exciting chase caught him in a corner by the greenhouse.

"Bad Toby! Bad Toby!" said Paul as he dragged him by the collar up toward the shed. "Toby mustn't run away from us anymore. Toby's going to have a nice bath."

Toby didn't appreciate the last remark at all. His tail had stopped wagging and his eyes had a strange, determined look.

It was quite a job to get him into the tub. Paul lifted his front legs and Barbara his back legs, and together they got him in. But it was quite another matter to *keep* him in. For a moment or two he stood quite still while Paul sponged his ears. Then all of a sudden he began to kick and jump and splash water all over.

"Hold him, Paul," cried Barbara, "or he'll jump out of the tub!"

"Can't you see I'm holding him as hard as I can?" said Paul. "You go on washing him."

Barbara began to wash him while Paul tried his best to keep Toby in the tub. Barbara got as far as covering Toby with a good lather of soap, when suddenly something happened.

For a moment Toby became very still. He seemed to forget that he was being bathed. His eyes had caught sight of something down in the yard. His back stiffened, his tail stood up, and with a loud "Yap, yap" he shook his collar free, leaped from the tub, and dashed away at top speed.

"Stop him!" cried Barbara helplessly, wiping the water from her dress and ankles.

"You'll never stop him!" said Paul. "Can't you see? There's Mrs. Tompkins' cat!"

"Oh dear!" cried Barbara. "I hope he doesn't hurt her."

There was no fear of that, since this particular kitty had often been chased by Toby, and knew every possible hiding place in both the yard and the house.

"Oh, look!" cried Barbara, as dog and cat raced back and forth across the flower beds, and in and out among the trees and bushes. "What a dreadful mess Toby will be!"

She was right. In the chase, Toby's soap-covered body gathered up mud, leaves, and bits of twigs, until he looked as if he'd never had a bath in his life.

"I just hope Daddy doesn't look out the window until we've got the little rascal cleaned up," said Paul.

"You're right," said Barbara.

But there was no need for them to worry about Daddy; he was still sleeping soundly, quite unconscious of what was going on outside.

"Now you can catch him," said Barbara as kitty made a sudden

turn and came rushing up the yard toward them, Toby close behind. "Grab him as he goes by."

But it was easier said than done. Paul made a grab, but his hand got only a greasy mixture of soap and mud, and away went Toby faster than ever.

"Look!" cried Barbara. "Look where the cat's going."

Growing tired and hunting for a safe place to hide, kitty had seen the half-open window of the living room. With a mighty spring she leaped onto the window sill, dropped down inside, and dived under an armchair that was pulled up near the fireplace.

Paul and Barbara held their breath. Would Toby follow? Could he possibly jump so high?

"Toby! Toby!" they both shrieked, hoping to call him off the chase.

But Toby didn't hear. With a jump bigger than he'd ever made before, Toby got his paws up on the window sill and scrambled over. He was in the living room. Dirty, muddy, soapy Toby was in the living room!

Toby forgot all about the cat when he saw his master in the easy chair. He jumped up in his usual friendly way onto the sleeping form. Waking with a start, Daddy found his arms full of a strange, warm, wriggling, soapy mass.

"*What'll* we do?" said Paul. "Daddy'll be awfully cross with us."

"There's only one thing to do," said Barbara. "We'd better go in right now and say we're sorry."

"All right," said Paul. "I'll come with you."

As they reached the living room, the French doors opened and out came Toby, even more quickly than he had gone in. Daddy stood inside. He looked very stern. His clothes were a terrible sight, covered with soapy dirt!

"We're dreadfully sorry," said Barbara. "We never dreamed he would do it, and we'll clean up all the mess and brush your trousers and everything. Please forgive us."

Daddy looked at the two children and down at his clothes. Then his face broke into the least bit of a smile.

"Oh, you two terrible children!" he said. "But I suppose I'll have to forgive you again."

And Paul and Barbara put their arms around his neck and hugged him ever so tight.

Unlucky Jim

JIM THOUGHT he was the most unlucky boy who had ever been born. Everything seemed to be going wrong. Life looked particularly dark at the moment, because his only glass marble had just rolled down a drain.

But besides that, he had a lot of reasons to feel blue. He was shivering with cold. He should have had warm socks and under-clothes to wear, but he didn't have any. His dad was out of work and didn't have enough money to buy them.

He was hungry, too. It had been a long time since lunch, and the bread and butter he'd had then seemed to have gone clear down to the South Pole. As Jim trudged along the streets with his hands in his pockets, he saw lots of other boys and girls going into beauti-ful homes for their supper, and he knew that he would have to climb up the dirty, narrow stairs of a dingy, crowded apartment building

for the little bit of bread he would get.

Just then he passed a toy shop blazing with lights and full of everything that could make a boy's heart glad. Jim stopped a moment and watched other boys and girls coming out carrying all sorts of interesting packages.

Jim jabbed his hand deeper into his pocket and fingered his nickel again, his very last coin. How he wished he could buy something to take to his little sister, lying at home so sick. If only he could get her something she would really like.

"If I ain't the unluckiest fellow that ever lived!" he said to himself.

142

But the next day his luck changed. He was walking down the
street when a well-dressed woman stopped and spoke to him. "Is
your name Jimmie Mackay?" she asked.

"Yes, ma'am," said Jimmie, surprised, and wondering what was
going to happen.

"Well," said the woman, "we have your name on a list at our
church, and we want you to come to a special Christmas party next
week. Here is a ticket for you."

"Oh, boy!" said Jimmie, not knowing what else to say. "But what
about Jean—she's my sister, y' know; she'll be better by then.

Perhaps—she ought t' come too."

"I'm afraid we can take only one from each family this time," said the woman kindly. "We'll try to take Jean next time."

"Well, that's lucky and unlucky," said Jim to himself as the woman walked away. "Lucky for me and unlucky for Jean."

Then a bright idea occurred to him. Maybe he could let Jean go instead of him. He looked at his card. It read "Admit bearer—Jimmie Mackay—only."

"Unlucky again!" murmured Jimmie.

So Jimmie went to the party. Most of the time he forgot all about his troubles. Everything was so different, so very wonderful. He had never, ever had so much to eat.

After the meal they all played games until it was time for the presents on the Christmas tree to be given away. Everyone was excited, because each child would be able to choose just what he or she wanted most.

Jim could hardly sit still as he watched the other children going up in front of him. He felt as if he were on pins and needles. He had seen a wonderful toy fire engine hanging on the tree—something he had wanted all his life. How he hoped and hoped and *hoped* that no one else would ask for it first!

At last, after what seemed hours, Jimmie's turn came to make his choice. "Jimmie Mackay!" called out the woman by the tree.

Jimmie jumped from his seat like a shell from a cannon. All he could see was the red fire truck. It was still there!

As he approached the woman he noticed that she was the same one who had spoken to him in the street and given him his ticket for the party. Just then he had a bright idea.

"And what would you like to have, Jimmie?" asked the woman. "You may have any one thing you like from the tree."

What an offer! Jimmie could hardly believe it. He stood and

144

gazed up at the sparkling, heavily laden tree. He caught sight of the fire truck.

"Most of all," he said, looking up at the lady, "I would like that red fire truck; but if you don't mind, I'll take that doll over there." Tears filled his eyes as he said it, but with great resolution he kept his face straight.

Somehow the woman seemed to understand, and without a word she brought Jimmie the doll. As he went away, she squeezed his hand. Bending down, she whispered, "God bless you, Jimmie."

But the other children didn't understand at all. There were giggles and snickers, then whoops and yells as they told the world that Jimmie had chosen a doll! Some of the boys called out, "Sissy!" and others said with a laugh, "Imagine a boy taking a doll!" The little girls said, "That was just the doll we wanted!"

Jimmie blushed. He couldn't help it. Finally he became so uncomfortable that he put on his cap and went out with the doll under his arm.

All the way home he thought about the bad luck that seemed to have dogged his footsteps. First, he had lost his fire truck, and second, he had been laughed at by the whole crowd of children.

"If I ain't the unluckiest fellow—" he began. Then he felt the doll under his arm. Immediately his thoughts brightened and his step quickened. A few minutes later he was up in the little dark bedroom where Jean lay sick in bed.

"I'm so glad you've come!" said Jean. "It's so lonely here all by myself. And what do you have there?" she asked, sitting up in bed and peering eagerly at the doll. "Is that for me? Oh, Jimmie, Jimmie, you *are* a dear!"

Jimmie forgot all about his bad luck. A thrill of joy went through him as he saw his sister's delight.

Just then there was a knock at the door. It was the woman from the church. "What—" began Jimmie.

"I've come to say how sorry I am that the children were so un-kind to you this evening," interrupted the woman. "They are sorry too, now. I told them why you chose the doll. And they asked me to bring you something for yourself. Here it is. Now I must go, for it is getting late. Good night!" and she was gone.

Jimmie gasped, and then opened the package.

It was the fire engine!

Then he danced a jig around Jean's bed, chuckling to himself and saying, "If I ain't the luckiest fellow alive!"

Bag It

Do you need an inexpensive gift idea that will work for just about everybody on your Christmas list? Make some shoe bags. Shoe bags are good for anyone who travels and hates to pack dirty shoes with his or her clothes, but they are useful in many other ways, too. Fill them with nuts in the shell, candy, ribbon and lace scraps for making doll clothes, or small scraps of wood for your little brother to stack and glue.

To make two shoe bags large enough for your dad's shoes, you will need four pieces of material each 10 inches by 18 inches. You can make smaller bags for other purposes. If you want to decorate the bags, decorate the pieces of material before you sew them into bags.

For each bag, put two pieces of material right sides together. Sew around three edges. Fold the top edge down a quarter inch to the inside of the bag, and sew. Fold it down another inch, to make a pocket for a string or ribbon you will use as a drawstring, and sew, leaving an opening for the drawstring. Use a safety pin to thread the string or ribbon through the pocket. The bags make nice gifts by themselves, or you can fill 'em up!

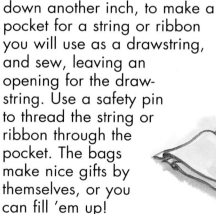

Boasting Billy

WILLIAM Arnold Croker, known to the other boys in the town as "Billy," was a bright boy, but he had one fault. He thought so much of himself that his hat would hardly go on his head.

Billy's skill in games made him a natural leader of the boys, but they all secretly disliked him because he was always bragging about the wonderful things he could do. Instead of listening to what the other boys had to say, he interrupted them with a story of some experience he had had. If someone said he had seen a big frog, Billy would say, "That's nothing; last week I saw a frog much bigger than that."

At last the other boys got tired of his boasting, and began to talk about some way of putting an end to it. As Tyler Walters said, Billy was swollen up with pride as big as a balloon, and it was high time somebody stuck a pin into him.

But how to do it was another question. Some of the boys sug-

149

gested ducking him in the river; but Billy was a strong boy, and none of the others wanted to take the risk of a personal quarrel with him. Then Tyler struck on a bright idea.

"I know of something better than that," he said. "It wouldn't be kind to put him in the river, and it wouldn't do him much good anyway. Have you ever thought about what is the matter with Billy?"

The others crowded around. "No, what?" they asked. They were in a mood to try anything.

"I'll tell you. You've all noticed how Billy seems to win all our games," said Tyler. "That's the trouble with him. He thinks we're no good, and he can always beat us. If we're going to stop his bragging, we'll have to learn to play better ourselves."

"Pretty good sense," said another boy. "If Billy lost some games, he would change his tune."

"You're right," said Tyler, "but it's up to us to beat him. Why not practice some of our games on the sly, and surprise Billy?"

"But we can't all win," said a pale-faced, timid youngster. "And I don't see how we can practice all the games we play."

"Of course we can't all practice everything at once," said Tyler. "But one or two of us can practice running, some of us can work on jumping, and others can shoot baskets. I'm going to practice so I can throw him out at first base the next time we play."

"Great!" laughed the others. "Let's do it."

Tyler's idea certainly put new life into those boys. Their mothers and teachers began to wonder what was the matter with them, because nearly all of them began to practice hard at the games they had chosen in their secret meeting.

Tyler began to practice batting and fielding every morning and evening. In the morning, before his father went to work, Tyler would get him out into the vacant lot next to the house to pitch him a few balls.

After school he would get one of the boys to play with him. Then in the evening after supper his father would throw him a few more, until his eye and timing were nearly perfect, and he could hit curves as hard as straight balls.

Billy began to notice a difference in how the boys played. He had always been able to keep an easy lead in races, but a few of the boys were beginning to keep up with him. He never dreamed, however, that the boys were working hard to beat him.

School field day came around, full of races and games. Billy hadn't bothered to practice for any of the events because he felt so certain of success. The other boys, however, had worked very hard

Fred Collins

with just one purpose in view. And their hard work paid off. They won. Poor Billy didn't win a single race.

Billy felt very bad about it. But he was counting on the baseball game that came at the end of the day to save his reputation. This ball game was always a big affair, at least in the boys' eyes. It was held

on the town diamond, and usually there were lots of spectators. Billy was an excellent hitter, and he was determined to come out a hero.

Billy was up first. "Look out, boys," he cried. "You'd better keep your eye on the town clock, 'cause I'm going to hit a ball right in the middle of it." Carrying his bat with a real swagger, he strolled

across the field as if he were a professional. But much to his surprise, Billy fanned out.

In the next inning Tyler was up first. His great opportunity had come. After all he had said to the other boys, he knew what he had to do.

Tyler walked out to the batter's box. The pitcher shot him a fast ball. But Tyler was ready; he had been training his eye carefully, and he was sure of his swing. To everyone's surprise, he hit the ball far out into the field. Before the left fielder recovered the ball, Tyler was rounding third. The left fielder threw to Billy, who was catching, but Billy dropped the ball, and Tyler slid in home—a home run.

Tyler made two more home runs that day. He hit the last one in the last inning with two out and two men on base, partly because Billy, who was really a good player, lost his nerve when someone

154

else played better than he, and partly because Tyler had worked so
hard to succeed.

At the close of the game all the boys crowded around Tyler and
proclaimed him hero of the day. With a heavy heart, Billy watched
them from the edge of the field.

"How about the town clock?" piped a small voice behind him.

Billy turned red. "Maybe next time," he mumbled.

That was the last "pin" Billy needed to have stuck into him.
Every time he was tempted to boast after that, he remembered the
town clock, and swallowed his words.

Constellations

Big Dipper

Little Dipper

Something about looking at the stars shows us what a very small part of the universe we are! Theodore Roosevelt had a ritual he followed before he went to bed. He would find a patch of light near the constellation Pegasus. "That is the Spiral Galaxy in Andromeda," he would say. "It's as large as our Milky Way. It is one of hundreds of millions of galaxies. It consists of 100 billion suns, each larger than our sun." When he felt small enough, he would go to bed!

You can make a device to practice identifying constellations. Use a round oatmeal box, black construction paper, and a flashlight. Cut the center out of the lid of the oatmeal box, leaving about an inch of rim. Punch holes for each constellation you want to learn in a circle of black paper, cut to fit inside the lid of the oatmeal box. Put the lid on the box, and shine the flashlight inside the box, throwing the pinpoints of light showing the constellation on the ceiling or wall.

Four Jars of Jam

JESSICA and Dawna had just returned home from the big city. They were very excited and very tired, though they wouldn't admit it, for they had spent the whole day with Mom walking around a wonderful exhibition. It had been such fun! They had seen so many interesting things that when they began to tell Daddy about them they got all mixed up.

Then they began to bring out the treasures they had gathered during the day. Both of them had a collection of the most delightful little samples you could wish to see—tiny pieces of cheese wrapped in silver paper, packages of cookies and cornflakes, and, best of all, four dainty little jars of jam.

Oh, those jars of jam! What shrieks of delight greeted their unpacking! How pretty they looked, standing on the table with the light shining through them. One was strawberry jam, one apricot

jam, one blackberry jelly, and the other marmalade.

Jessica and Dawna took a long time to decide how the four jars should be divided, but at last Jessica agreed to have the strawberry and the apricot, and Dawna took the blackberry jelly and the marmalade.

Imagine having two whole jars of jam each! It seemed too wonderful to be true. Jessica and Dawna put them beside their plates at suppertime so they could keep their eyes on them. Of course, they weren't very big, but to Jessica and Dawna they were more precious than the biggest in Mother's cupboard.

All through suppertime they talked about their four treasured jam jars—how they got them, and what they were going to do with them. They were quite sure they were going to eat all the jam themselves, and that if they tasted only a spoonful every day the jars would last for weeks and weeks.

Supper was almost over when Daddy said something that upset things a bit.

"Poor old Dad!" he said, talking sadly to himself. "Poor old Dad!

158

He never has a jam jar all to himself. Nobody ever gives him anything. Poor old Dad!"

Jessica and Dawna stopped talking. They both looked at Daddy in surprise, wondering whether he really meant what he said. Then they looked at their precious jam jars.

"Here, Daddy," said Jessica, "have my jar of strawberry jam."

"You darling girl!" said Daddy. "I don't want to take your jam. I was just teasing."

"But you must have it," said Jessica, setting the jar of strawberry jam down with a bang in front of Daddy's plate. "You see, I still have the apricot left."

Daddy nearly shed a tear at this, but he didn't because he was too busy watching Dawna out of the corner of his eye.

The struggle was harder for Dawna. She was breathing deeply and looking hard at one jar and then at the other. She picked up the marmalade, put it down, then picked up the blackberry jelly. Her solemn little face showed that a big battle was being fought inside.

"Daddy," she said at last, "I think I will let you have one of mine as well. You can have this jar of blackberry jelly."

And with that Dawna plumped the jar of blackberry jelly down beside Daddy's plate.

"You dear, precious girls," said Daddy. "Of course I won't eat your lovely jam; but I'm glad you gave it to me. I'll remember it forever and ever."

The Boy Who Brought Heaven Nearer

IT ALL began in a church in Italy. Forgetting the music and the prayers, a boy kept his eyes fixed on a swinging lamp. Someone had just lit it, then left it swinging on its chain.

As the lamp swung back and forth, young Galileo noticed that it took as long to swing in a wide arc as in a small arc. Not having a watch, he timed it with his pulse and found he was right. This was something new. He had always thought it would take longer for a pendulum to cover the greater distance.

As soon as he got home from church that day he fixed up a pendulum of his own, set it going, and found that it worked the same way. Then he made more pendulums of different lengths and weights, hanging them from ceiling beams and boughs of trees till

161

his family thought he must be crazy. But he proved his point. And this started him on the road to many other discoveries.

Galileo loved to experiment. He wouldn't accept anybody else's word for something, but set out to prove things for himself.

The schools in his day taught that if two weights were dropped from a high place, the heavier object would hit the ground first. Galileo questioned this. He tried dropping weights from high places and found it wasn't true. All weights released together hit the ground at the same time. But nobody would believe him.

One day he persuaded a group of university professors to go with him to the top of the famous Leaning Tower of Pisa. From there he dropped a 10-pound weight and a one-pound weight together. Both hit the ground exactly at the same moment. The professors were amazed, but they still wanted to believe their books instead of their eyes!

In 1609 Galileo made his greatest discovery. A rumor reached him that a Dutch eyeglass maker's assistant, holding two glass lenses a foot or so apart, had noticed that they made things appear larger. Immediately Galileo set out to prove whether the story was true. He set up two lenses a foot apart and got the same result. Then he took larger lenses, put them together, and made the first telescope.

News about his invention soon spread, but many people scoffed and said it couldn't be so. Then Galileo took his telescope to the top of the Campanile, the highest tower in Venice. With him went many of the leading people of the city, including senators, dressed in rich robes as if they were attending an important ceremony. What they saw astounded them. Through Galileo's telescope they could see the streets of Padua, 20 miles away, and people walking in them. A ship 50 miles away seemed no farther than five miles. Again and again they looked through the telescope and marveled.

After that Galileo began making telescopes for sale. People from all over Europe bought them. He made one for himself which he called "Old Discoverer." It made objects appear 33 times nearer.

One night—and that was a very great night in history—he turned his telescope on the heavens. The glorious scene startled him. Instead of seeing just a few stars, like we see with the naked eye, he saw thousands and thousands of them. The Milky Way, which most people had thought of as a misty veil, was really a gorgeous band of stars.

Suddenly Galileo realized that the universe was not just the earth, the sun, the moon, and a few pinpoints of light called stars, but something infinitely greater and more marvelous. The darkness of space was lit with blazing orbs as far as human eyes could see!

Galileo turned his telescope on Jupiter and found that the three bright stars in line with it were not stars at all but moons, moving around the planet, just like our moon moves around the earth.

Looking at the sun through darkened lenses, he saw a huge ball of fire with dark clouds moving over it, which today we call sunspots. He noticed, too, that the sun was moving on its axis, just as the earth does.

This was too wonderful. He was thrilled. He longed to tell others, and he did. But people wouldn't believe him. Church leaders told him he had to be wrong. The things he had seen were so different from what they had always believed that they were sure he couldn't be right. They had him arrested and put in prison so he couldn't teach his "false" ideas.

But Galileo was right, and he knew it. He knew, too, that others would look through the telescopes he had built and prove that he was right.

And that's what happened. As years and centuries rolled by, bigger and bigger telescopes were built, each one proving not only that

what Galileo taught was true but also showing that the universe is even bigger than he imagined.

Maybe you have read about the Hubble Space Telescope, the most expensive ever built. The U.S. space shuttle *Discovery* carried it into orbit around the earth. It was designed to see things in space 10 times more clearly than telescopes on earth because it is out of the earth's atmosphere. The Hubble had a number of problems which astronauts have fixed; and it is returning some spectacular images of new wonders in the skies around us.

When you think of this, remember Galileo, the boy who watched the swinging lamp in the church. By inventing the telescope, he opened up many secrets of God's marvelous universe and brought heaven nearer to earth.

Magnifiers

To *magnify* something means to make it look bigger. When you look at your thumb under a magnifying glass, it doesn't grow bigger, but it looks bigger. The glass takes the light that you are using to see your thumb and spreads it out over a wider area, so your thumb seems to cover a wider area too.

Can you think of other things that magnify? Look at your feet while you are standing in a swimming pool. The water makes them look big! A telescope is a magnifier, and so are binoculars.

Try this finger play.

Binoculars make things look near (circle eyes with fingers)

So feathers on a bird are clear.

I use my telescope at night (double fists together)

So stars look bigger, and more bright.

A magnifying glass is fun (make big circle with fingers)

Because it helps me watch ants run.

But what use would these three things be (spread hands, palm up)

If I didn't have two eyes that see! (point to eyes)

Harry's Motorboat

THE GREAT dream of Harry's life had come true. For years and years, so it seemed, Harry had longed for a model motorboat that really worked, and now at last he had one. Only this morning his uncle had brought him the boat as a birthday present.

What happiness!

First of all, of course, it had to be tried out in the bathtub, just to see whether it really would go. But after Harry had seen it go up and down the tub a score of times he couldn't wait until he had taken it to the lake.

Carefully holding his precious little boat, he proudly started off toward the park.

"You *will* be careful, won't you?" said Mother.

"Of course," promised Harry.

"And be sure to be back by six o'clock?"

167

"Yes, Mother."

And away he went. What fun he had! What a thrill it was to put his boat into the water and start the motor.

Away went the little boat across the lake, while Harry rushed round in his bare feet to meet it at the other side. He was so excited that he walked into the water to meet it coming in. Turning it round, he sent it off again, this time toward a different spot.

Time goes quickly when one is happy, and Harry didn't notice how the hours were slipping by. At last, however, he noticed the lengthening shadows, and he stopped a passerby to ask him the time.

"Half past five."

"Phew!" whistled Harry. "I'll have to be packing up soon. Just time for one more trip."

How often "one more trip" is really one too many! Anyway, that's what happened with Harry. For the last trip, he decided to send the boat on the longest possible journey across the lake. If the boat reached the point he aimed at, he thought, it would be near the footpath that led toward home. So, he argued, an extra long trip would really save time.

Away went the motorboat on her "transatlantic" crossing, with Harry watching her delightedly every inch of the way.

"She's halfway across!" he muttered to himself.

Then his heart seemed to stand still. The boat had stopped. What happened, he couldn't tell. Maybe he had used the boat too much. Perhaps it had caught in some reeds. Harry didn't know. He stood on the bank with eyes glued on the boat, hoping against hope that it would start again. But it didn't move. How could he get it back? Far in the distance he heard a factory whistle.

"That's the five-to-six whistle," he said to himself, "and I must be home at six!"

Poor Harry! What should he do? He must *keep* his promise to his mother, because he always did. But if he went away, someone might get the boat before he could return. In desperation he walked into the water as far as he could, but found that it suddenly became very deep just a few yards from the shore and he had to return.

Again he looked at the little boat quietly bobbing up and down in the middle of the lake. Then he thought of the time.

"Oh, what shall I do?" he said to himself.

No one was around who could help him, because the few who had been there in the afternoon had already gone home. Suddenly an unusual thought came into his mind. Some of you may smile when I tell you what it was. It was the music of a hymn he had sung in church a few days before. The words came back to him.

"What a friend we have in Jesus,
    All our sins and griefs to bear;

What a privilege to carry
Everything to God in prayer."

"But," Harry said to himself, "surely Jesus isn't interested in my little motorboat!" He almost smiled at the thought. Then in his desperate anxiety he said, "Why not? Perhaps He is."

And right there by the lakeside Harry shut his eyes for just a second and asked Jesus to look after his little boat while he ran home to keep his promise to his mother.

Taking one last, loving look at his precious boat, he turned away and ran home as fast as he could go. He was a few minutes late, but Mother said nothing about it, for she saw right away that he was very upset. When she learned that he had even left his boat behind in the lake in order to keep his promise to her she felt very proud of him.

"After supper," she said, "we'll both go back, even though it's dark, and see what we can do with a ball of string."

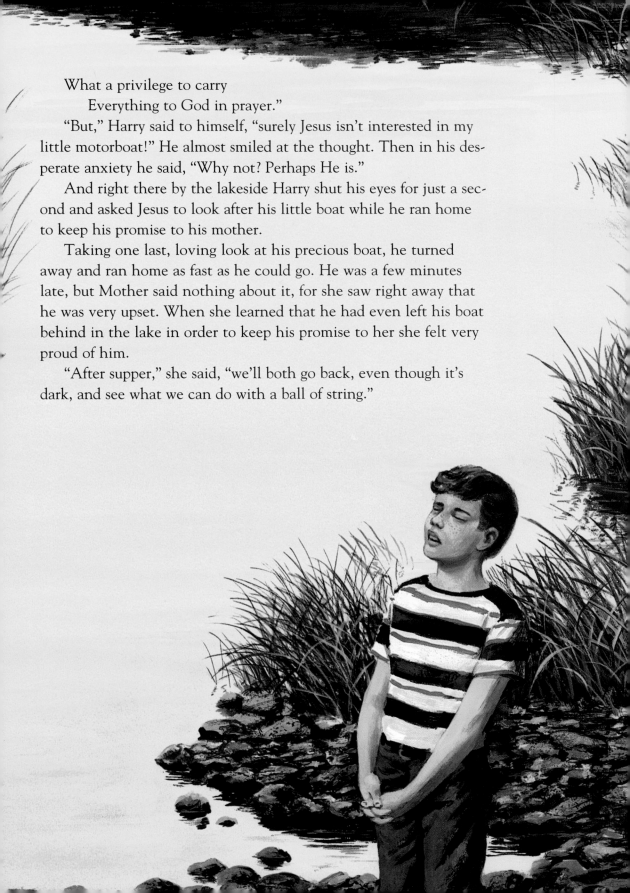

Supper didn't take long, I can assure you, and by seven Harry and his mother were on their way back to the lake with a flashlight and string enough to stretch across.

By the time they arrived, a pale moon was rising, casting its rays across the silent waters.

Eagerly they both strained their eyes, hoping to catch a glimpse of the little boat.

"It was over there," said Harry, "right in the middle."

"I can't see it," said Mother.

"Neither can I," said Harry with a trace of fear in his voice.

"Perhaps when the moon is a bit higher—" began Mother with a note of encouragement.

"No," said Harry disconsolately, "it's gone. I know just where it was. It must have sunk."

They walked all around the lake, hoping it might have drifted ashore. But there was no trace of it.

"There's no use looking anymore," sighed Harry. "Let's go home."

And in his heart he said, "And what was the good of asking Jesus to look after it?"

Crunch! Heavy footsteps nearby startled them both. "Hello!"

172

called a deep voice. "What are you doing here in the dark?"

It was the game warden.

"I lost my motorboat this afternoon," said Harry, "and Mother and I have come down to look for it."

"Have you found it?" asked the man more kindly.

"No, we haven't," said Harry.

"I wouldn't think you could in the dark," he said. "It's late now. You'd better follow me."

Something in his tone of voice raised Harry's hopes.

They turned and followed the man along the lakeshore until they reached an old boathouse. The game warden stopped, pulled out a bunch of keys, and opened the creaky door.

"Bring your flashlight over here," he said.

The beam from the flashlight fell on the precious motorboat!

"There it is, there it is!" cried Harry. "How did you get it out of the lake?"

"With my boat," said the game warden. "I saw it caught in the reeds and guessed some boy would be looking for it. So I just rowed out and brought it in."

"Thank you ever so much!" said Harry as he and Mother said good night. Then they hurried home, Harry gripping the motorboat as though he might lose it again.

On the way his heart sent up a silent thank You to the Friend who never forgets a request, and who even answers the prayer of a boy for his boat.

God's Hands

JABARI was working in his own garden on the compound of a mission school in West Africa. Very carefully he pulled out every weed he could find. Suddenly, as he worked, he became ill. Some of his friends took him to the mission hospital.

The nurse took his temperature, put him in bed, and called the doctor.

Jabari was terribly disappointed about being sick, because the superintendent would make his yearly inspection of all the gardens in only three weeks, and he had really hoped he would win the prize this year.

Every day he had worked hard, digging, planting, weeding, and doing his best to make his garden the nicest garden at the mission. But now all his hopes

seemed shattered. As he lay in the hospital he pictured the weeds growing up—they grow very quickly in West Africa—and spoiling all he had done.

Inspection day drew nearer, but Jabari was not allowed to get up. He knew there was no possible hope of his winning. The other boys would be working hard on their gardens and making them look all spic-and-span. He didn't stand a chance.

Meanwhile something was happening at the mission. Nuru, Jabari's friend, had a bright idea. He, too, was going in for the competition, but he thought it was too bad that Jabari didn't have a chance to win because of his illness.

He talked to the other boys about it, and they all agreed to give just a little time each day to keep the weeds out of Jabari's garden

175

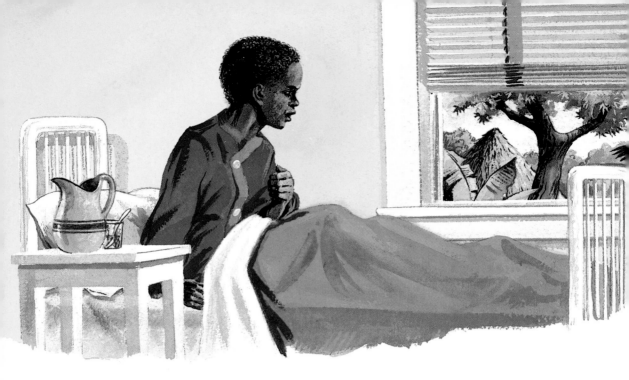

until the inspection. So while they still tried to make their own gardens the best, they each gave a little extra care and love to the sick boy's garden.

At last inspection day arrived. Jabari was still lying in the hospital, and he was discouraged. He thought he could see his garden covered with weeds. He pictured the superintendent walking through the gardens and saying, "Whose garden has all these dreadful weeds in it?" Then he seemed to hear some of the boys saying, "Oh, that's Jabari's garden."

It was too bad, he thought, that in spite of all his work—and he knew he had worked harder than the others—his garden would look like such a disgrace. But there was nothing he could do about it now.

Jabari was becoming more and more miserable when the door of the ward opened, and to his surprise in walked the superintendent

176

and a group of the boys. What was going on?

"We have come to congratulate you," said the superintendent, "for winning the prize for the best-kept garden this year."

"Me?" said Jabari, with eyes wide open.

"Yes, you," said the superintendent.

"But—but—it's all covered with weeds."

"It wasn't when I saw it this morning," said the superintendent.

"But—how—what?" began Jabari.

"It's all right," said Nuru with a twinkle in his eye. "We're all happy that you've won the prize. You see, God didn't let the weeds grow in your garden because you deserved to win; He knew you had worked harder than anyone else."

"I think that's right," said the superintendent, "but I believe He had some human hands to help Him."

All the boys laughed happily and ran out again to their work, while Jabari, overjoyed, blinked back tears of gladness.

When Work Needs to Be Done

Have you ever heard someone say, "That's not my job, so I won't do it" or "I didn't make that mess, so I won't clean it up"? Big-hearted people do jobs because they need doing, and they don't worry about whether they are working harder than someone else, or if someone else should be doing it instead.

During the American Revolution a group of exhausted soldiers were struggling to repair a wall of stone and dirt to protect them from enemy bullets. One soldier was shouting instructions, but made no move to help the others. An officer in plain clothing happened to ride by, and asked the man why he wasn't helping. "Sir," he retorted, "I am a corporal!"

The officer apologized, got down from his horse, and helped the soldiers himself. When the work was done, he turned to the corporal. "Mr. Corporal," he said, "next time you have a job like this and not enough men to do it, go to your commander in chief, and I will come and help you again." The corporal hadn't recognized General George Washington.

A Little Child Shall Lead Them

YOU MAY think this is a made-up story, but it isn't. It's absolutely true. I know the little boy and girl very well, and it was their mother who told it to me. I'll call the boy Donald and the girl Margaret. Margaret was 5, and Donald, $8\frac{1}{2}$.

One day when Mother was cleaning up the living room she threw a Christmas card on the fire. It was a very old one that had been sent to Margaret at least four years before.

It had just started to burn, when Margaret began to make a fuss. "That's my Christmas card," she cried. "You shouldn't have burned it. I've kept it all this time, and I want it."

"I'm sorry," Mother said, trying to make the matter right. "It was such a dirty card, and it has been lying around for so long I thought you didn't want it anymore."

"But of course I wanted it!" cried Margaret, getting more angry.

179

"You should have known I wanted it. Why would you burn my things, anyway?"

Mother tried calmly to explain to Margaret that she had lots of other cards, and soon it would be Christmas again when her friends would send her many more.

But Margaret refused to be reasoned with, and began calling her mother some very unkind names. Mother couldn't allow this, of course, and sent her to her room, and soon a sobbing little girl went upstairs and climbed into her bed.

Donald was in bed by now also, and when Mother had kissed them both good night and gone out of the room, he began to talk to his little sister. Mother, on the stairs, stopped to listen.

"Margaret," said Donald, "you must be a good girl and go to sleep."

"I can't go to sleep," said Margaret. "I've been so bad, and I don't want Mother to punish me anymore."

"I know," said Donald, with sympathy and wisdom beyond his years. "You have been very naughty, and it made me feel so sad and awful inside, but if you would just say a little prayer to Jesus, everything would be all right again."

"But I don't know what to say," said Margaret, in between the tears and sobs that shook her little body.

"If you like, Margaret, I'll help you," said Donald, "and you could say it after me. Do you want me to?"

"Yes, please."

There was a pause. Then Donald began. "Dear Lord Jesus. Now, Margaret, say it after me."

"Dear Lord Jesus," repeated Margaret.

"Help me not to be naughty," said Donald.

"Help me not to be naughty," repeated Margaret.

"Forgive me for showing so much temper tonight."

The sobs increased, and for a while Margaret didn't speak.

181

At last she repeated, "Forgive me for showing so much temper tonight."

"And help me to be a good little girl," continued Donald.

"And help me to be a good little girl," repeated Margaret.

"And please forgive all my sins. Thank You, dear Jesus. Amen," said Donald.

Margaret again repeated after him.

"Is that all now, Donald?" she asked.

"Yes," said Donald. "Don't cry anymore. You see, Jesus loves you and has already forgiven you. He will help you to do what is right if you ask Him. Doesn't that make you happy, Margaret?"

"Oh, yes, Donald. I feel better now. And Mother won't punish me anymore?"

"No, Margaret, of course not. You've asked Jesus to help you to be good, and if we're good, Mom and Dad are happy, and then they never have to punish us, do they?"

"No," said Margaret.

"Good night," said Donald.

"Good night, Donald," said Margaret. "I'm so glad it's all right now."

Then silence, while Mother crept softly downstairs with tears in her eyes and gladness in her heart, happy to know that her darlings had already found a friend in Jesus, and were learning so soon to ask for His help and forgiveness.

31

Three Wonderful Songs

WHAT better way can we end this book than with a story of angel songs?

Let your thoughts wander back over the years, back and back and back, before you were born, before Daddy was born, before Grandma was born, before there were any cars or buses or houses or animals. Everything is still and dark. Let's stand quietly and watch God making the world.

Suddenly a Voice, majestic and musical, rings through space: "Let there be light!" The darkness vanishes, and light breaks over the waste of waters. Again

the Voice is heard, and the sky is made, and the dry land rises from the waters, grass grows on the mountains and the valleys, and the trees spring up—apple trees, plum trees, pear trees, and all the beautiful trees in the woods.

Again and again the Voice is heard. The fish appear in the sea, the birds fly in the air, and the animals are created upon the land—cows, sheep, goats, lions, tigers, elephants, and giraffes.

At last the earth is fashioned into a beautiful home, with lovely lakes and rivers, tall trees, and pretty flowers. What a glorious place it must have been, fresh from the hands of God! I would like to have seen it, wouldn't you? What sweet apples must have grown on those first fruit trees, what delicious oranges, bananas, peaches, and grapes! And how beautiful those first dainty flowers must have been, the first buttercups, the first daisies, the first snow-white lilies, the first glorious daffodils, and the first sweet-scented hyacinths.

When everything was finished, it was as beautiful as the great

God of heaven could make it. He said, "Let us make man in our image, after our likeness." Then from the dust of the ground, with His wonderful creative power, God formed the first man and the first woman, the father and mother of all the people in the world. The Bible tells us "God created man in his own image, in the image of God he created him; male and female he created them" (Genesis 1:27, NIV).

And then, suddenly, as the living man and woman stood on their feet, tall and beautiful, and looked happily at the wonderful home that God had made for them, all heaven burst into song. With great eagerness the angels had watched each step in the process of creation, and now, in this supreme moment, they broke into a chorus of adoring praise to God. "The morning stars sang together and all the angels shouted for joy" (Job 38:7, NIV).

Can you hear them singing? How the mighty sound surges through the sky and rolls around the clouds! Rising and falling as the wind wafts the melody here and there, it grows stronger and deeper and richer as it sweeps to its climax and they sing: "Holy, holy, holy is the Lord Almighty; the whole earth is full of his glory" (Isaiah 6:3, NIV).

How long the angels sang I don't know, but I'm sure that when Adam and Eve did wrong, and sin came in to spoil their beautiful home, they must have wept in disappointment. And as they saw the people of the world become more and more wicked and disobedient

as the years passed by, their sorrow must have been very deep. Their only comfort was found in the promise that one day their beloved Leader would go down to earth, and somehow recover what had been lost, and turn men's hearts back to God.

The next wonderful song was sung at the birth of Jesus, a very long time afterward. Did it seem long to the angels? Perhaps. Anyway, they must have wondered many times just how and when the promise was going to be fulfilled.

At last the time came. As they watched in amazement, their Leader went down to the world, not in power and glory but as a little baby. Eagerly they followed every detail of the plan. Then one night they gathered around Bethlehem in tens of thousands.

When the wonderful news flashed to the waiting angels that Jesus was born at last, their hearts thrilled with joy. They had to tell somebody, so they appeared to shepherds taking care of their sheep in the field, the only people who were ready to listen.

"The angel said to them, 'Do not be afraid. I bring you good news of great joy that will be for all the people. Today in the town of David a Savior has been born to you; he is Christ the Lord' " (Luke 2:10, 11, NIV).

The astonished shepherds looked up to see a glorious vision of angels spread across the sky, and they heard such angelic music no mortal had ever heard before.

"Glory to God in the highest, and on earth peace to men" (verse 14, NIV).

"Glory! Glory!" Can you hear them singing? How the glorious melody echoes from mountain to mountain and rolls out into the farthest reaches of space! "Glory! Glory!" Louder and louder grows the shout of praise, till it seems all heaven and earth must hear. Then fainter and fainter and still more faint as the vision fades, and the shepherds are left alone with their sheep and the stars again.

Almost 2,000 years have passed since then. Two thousand years! The angels have had to wait a long time to see their dream come true! Jesus didn't suddenly save the world, as they had hoped. He didn't set Himself up as a king and reign on the earth. Instead, He let Himself be led to the cross.

The angels had to stand by and see their beloved Leader ill-treated and mocked and beaten and killed. How many times they must have wanted to step in and save Him from His enemies! And when He told the people once that He could call 12 legions of angels to help Him if He wanted to, how they must have wished that He would!

But no, Jesus went to the cross and died, for He knew that was the only way to bring men back to God.

Many times during His earthly life Jesus told His disciples that after making His sacrifice He would leave them and come back again someday. He even told them about some of the signs that would let them know when He was about to return.

HERBERT
RUDEEN

I am sure the angels listened to every word He said. For 2,000 years they have been watching for the promised signs, and have been longing for the day when their Lord and Master will come back to the earth and complete His wonderful plans for those who love Him.

Someday—not very long from now—Jesus will return. When He comes, we are told, "all the angels" will come with Him. Won't that be a wonderful sight! Perhaps you and I will be alive to see it. Who knows? And then, if we love Jesus with all our hearts, the angels will take us to meet Him in the air. You can almost feel the thrill of it now, can't you? And then, along with the angels, we shall go to heaven to see all the beautiful things that God has prepared for those who love Him.

And on that glorious day we will hear music more wonderful than we have ever heard—the third wonderful song. Listen to the triumph song of the angels. It is the song they have been waiting to sing for so long. Their pent-up feelings will find freedom at last in this great chorus. Listen! The lovely strains of melody are coming toward us even now: "To him who sits on the throne and to the Lamb be praise and honor and glory and power, for ever and ever!" (Revelation 5:13, NIV).

Jesus has won the battle against sin and disease and death at last. Finally all that is evil and wicked has been left behind and destroyed. Never again will there be any quarreling or fighting or unkind words. Always and always there will be peace and joy and happiness. Jesus will be with His children forever.

Don't you want to join in that lovely song and live in that glorious home? I do. Let's plan to meet there, shall we?

The Piñata

In Latin America, Posada comes before Christmas and lasts nine days. Each night of Posada, children carry figures of Mary and Joseph through the house, stopping at each door and begging to enter. When they reach the room containing the stable, they put the figures inside. On Christmas Eve they put a figure of Baby Jesus in the manger. After this enactment come fun and games, and the children help break a piñata (pronounced **peen YAH tuh**), a hanging container filled with goodies.

You can make a piñata with papier-mâché. Soak newspaper strips in water. Make a paste out of flour and water, dip the wet newspaper into this paste, and plaster several layers around a balloon you have blown up. Don't put on too many layers, or the piñata will be hard to break.

Use toilet paper tubes for legs, and a smaller blown-up balloon to give shape to the head. Attach legs and head with paper-mâché strips, and allow to dry. Cut a hole in the top of your creation, and remove the balloon. Decorate your piñata with paint or fringed crepe paper, and fill it with small items such as nuts, balloons, stickers, and candy. Hang the piñata so even the smallest members of your family can take a turn at breaking it.